M000118357

WELCOME HOME

WELCOME HOME

SCRIPTURE, PRAYERS, AND BLESSINGS FOR THE HOUSEHOLD

YEAR OF MARK

Augsburg Fortress
Minneapolis

WELCOME HOME
Scripture, Prayers, and Blessings for the Household, Year of Mark

Sources of prayers and other seasonal materials are acknowledged on pages 162–165.

Editors: Samuel Torvend, Kari Kloos
Cover design: Lecy Design
Interior design: Marti Naughton
Contributors: Gordon Lathrop, Shawn Madigan, Craig Mueller, Gail Ramshaw, Martin Seltz, Alice Kjesbu Torvend

Manufactured in the U.S.A.   ISBN 0-8066-2840-5   10-28405

        01   00   99   98   97   96   1   2   3   4   5   6   7   8

Table of Contents

Introduction

How to use this book

When you have time, read the brief introductions to Daily Prayer and Sunday. Each introduction sets forth the various possibilities for prayer in the household. At the beginning of each season, read the introduction for that time of the year. Each of the nine seasonal introductions sets forth the meaning of that time of the year.

THREE PATTERNS OF PRAYER

Daily prayer contains short forms of prayer for use at various times: waking, morning, midday, evening, and going to bed. Though the patterns of prayer presented here begin with morning and end with nighttime, the reader is free to use whatever is helpful, given the diverse situations that mark contemporary household life.

For Christians, Sunday is the Lord's day, when the community of faith gathers at the table of the Word of God and the table of the holy supper. From the very beginning, Christians have set this day apart with prayer in the home. This book offers two patterns of **Sunday prayer**, one for the morning and another for the evening.

During the seasons of the year, the daily or Sunday pattern of prayer can be filled with new songs, psalms, and blessings. The pattern of **seasonal prayer** allows the household to experience the church's cycle of feasts and seasons that offer new images, customs, and cherished household practices. In this book, seasonal prayer begins with Advent (December) and ends with November.

TABLE PRAYER

At mealtime, use the Sunday or seasonal table prayer. Read the seasonal invitation, pause for a moment, and then pray the table prayer. The household is free to expand upon this simple meal blessing by lighting candles, singing a song, or listening to a brief passage from scripture.

SONG

Songs have been included for morning, evening, and bedtime prayer, Sunday, and each season of the year. While the hymn or song may be used at the beginning of prayer, it can be sung or read at any time of the day or season. Familiar tunes are noted at the end of each hymn text. If more than one person will be singing, it will be helpful to have copies of this book available for group use.

THE PSALMS

For hundreds of years, the psalms have been the prayerbook of Jews and Christians. By praying the psalms, contemporary Christians learn to pray with their spiritual ancestors, with Christ, and with the communion of saints. The psalm translations in this book are from the International Committee on English in the Liturgy (ICEL) and from the New Revised Standard Version (NRSV) of the Bible. If you use this book by yourself, slowly pray the psalm silently or out loud. If more than one person prays the psalm, the verses may be prayed alternately.

SCRIPTURE

With each season, the Sunday lectionary readings are printed in this book. In addition to the Sunday readings, a table of daily readings is printed for the week. This list of daily readings is rooted in and expands upon the scripture readings from the previous Sunday. In this way, the images, actions, and words of Sunday flow into the week.

The scripture readings may be read silently for personal reflection or out loud when a group of persons are gathered for prayer. The privilege of reading the Word of God may be shared among those who gather for prayer. After the reading, keep silence for a time so that the words may find a place to dwell in memory and the imagination. Resist the temptation to fill the silence with noise.

SCRIPTURE-RELATED PRAYERS

For each week of the year, two prayers based on the Sunday readings are provided. There is a brief prayer, easily memorized, that can be prayed throughout the day. These short biblical invocations are easily learned by children so that from an early age, the words of scripture become a part of the child's daily vocabulary. A prayer for use throughout the week offers a brief summary of the Sunday's Gospel reading.

CANTICLE

Since the early centuries of the church, Christians have prayed the Song of Zechariah (the Benedictus) in the morning, the Song of Mary (the Magnificat) in the evening, and the Song of Simeon (the Nunc dimittis) at night or at bedtime. Throughout the world today, millions of Christians sing or recite these central songs of the New Testament in hundreds of different languages. When we use these canticles, we join our voices to those of other Christians in distant lands.

In addition to these cherished canticles, this book offers Sunday and seasonal canticles for use in the home. Use the daily or seasonal canticle, or alternate between them in longer seasons.

PRAYER

Each pattern—daily, Sunday, and seasonal—provides an opportunity for prayer. Following the pattern of Sunday worship, household prayer moves from personal and/or family concerns to the larger circle of intercession for the community, the nation, and those in particular need. The Lord's Prayer and a seasonal or weekly prayer may conclude the prayers.

BLESSINGS FOR VARIOUS OCCASIONS AND PERSONS

Throughout the seasons, various blessings are included in this book. These blessings are related to household customs (such as the lighting of Advent candles), days (such as Christmas), or a particular need (such as travel). Anyone in the household who is capable of doing so, may read the prayer of blessing. When it is appropriate, the prayer of blessing may be expanded with the singing of a song, reading a passage from scripture, and/or praying the Lord's Prayer.

CHURCH YEAR CALENDAR FOR THE YEAR OF MARK

The Sunday scripture readings in this book follow the Revised Common Lectionary for Year B, in which the the Gospels of Mark and John are prominent. In the back of this book, a calendar lists the years and dates in which this cycle of readings will be used in the churches. This book may be used in these years: 1996–97, 1999–2000, 2002–2003, 2005–2006, 2008–2009.

Basic elements of Christian prayer in the home

In words and actions, the household can become a spiritual center where faith, hope, and love flourish in good times and in bad. This does not happen, however, through wishful thinking. Whether one lives alone or with others, it is important to cultivate a simple pattern of daily and seasonal prayer. Christians are intentional about fostering household prayer, not because God needs it or demands it, but because the words and songs, the customs and prayers of the household can lead one to see all of life from the perspective of faith. God has become one with our time, our place, our daily lives through the incarnation of the Son. In the pattern of Jesus' prayer, in his words and gestures, Christians see the way God invites us to live in our time and in our homes.

WHEN WE PRAY

The first Christians, being Jews, followed the patterns of prayer present in their religion and culture. They filled the patterns, however, with the life of Jesus Christ. Thus, since the earliest days, Christians have prayed in **the morning, at midday, in the evening, and at bedtime**. The images of the day—sunrise, noon, sunset, nightime—became ways to understand the presence of Christ throughout the day. And so Christians speak and sing of Christ the light who never sets, Christ the dawning light of God's mercy.

In the middle of the night, Christ rose from the dead and appeared to his followers on Sunday, the first day of the week: he opened the scriptures to them, he offered them his peace, he broke bread and shared a cup with them, he sent them forth into the world to proclaim the good news in word and act. For Christians, **Sunday is the day of Christ's resurrection** when the people of God gather to hear Christ speak in the scriptures, to celebrate baptism, to receive his peace, and to share his bread and cup with each other.

The center of the Christian year is the **Three Days of Maundy/Holy Thursday, Good Friday, and Holy Saturday/Easter Sunday** during which believers celebrate Christ's passover from suffering and death to risen life. The Easter Vigil/Easter Sunday is the primary baptismal festival of the year. The **Forty Days of Lent** invite the Christian community to examine its faithfulness to God's promises in baptism, to turn away from sin and receive God's mercy. In the **Fifty**

Days of Easter, Christians joyously celebrate the presence of the risen Christ and ask what it means to be his followers in public life.

The Christmas season draws our attention to the ever-present Christ who is our Word and our light. During **Advent**, we prepare to welcome the light. We listen to the prophets who announce God's reign of justice and peace. During the **Twelve Days of Christmas** we celebrate the presence of the Word-made-flesh who is Emmanuel, God with us. The festival of the **Epiphany** marks Christ's manifestation to the nations of the earth and invites Christians to participate in the church's global outreach. The Baptism of the Lord marks the beginning of Jesus' public ministry.

The many **Sundays after Pentecost** correspond to **Summer** and the first two months of **Autumn**. From the feast of All Saints to Christ the King/Reign of Christ, the Sunday readings during **November** draw us to contemplation of the last things: the communion of saints, the resurrection of the dead, and the life of the world to come.

These many feasts and seasons influence the daily and weekly practice of prayer. They present a rhythm that shapes the Christian awareness of God's presence in all seasons of the year and all seasons of human life. They invite us to celebrate this merciful presence in the many customs of the household.

WHERE WE PRAY

Prayer and reading may take place anywhere in the home: in a bedroom, out in the garden or yard, around the table, in the living room. For many people, it is important to have some visual focus or place for prayer: a cross or crucifix, a burning candle, a sacred image or icon. Throughout the seasons of the year, the place of prayer can vary: around the Advent wreath, close to the Christmas tree, next to a nativity scene, near a cross, around a bowl of water or vase of flowers, in the light of a burning candle.

When visiting the sick or homebound, bring *Welcome Home* with you. When traveling or on vacation, pack *Welcome Home* in your bag. If you are going to a hospital or nursing home, take *Welcome Home* with you. For a visit to a cemetery, use the words of *Welcome Home*.

HOW WE PRAY

We learn the words of faith and their many meanings by speaking them, listening to them, praying them, singing them. We also learn the words of faith by letting them speak in **silence**. The reading of scripture invites us to be quiet so that we might truly hear the Word speaking within us.

The faithful people of God pray for the needs of the Christian community, the nation and the world, the sick and dying, and the poor and needy. The needs of the day or the particular time in which we live are brought before God. It is that time when we can speak the truth, trusting in God's mercy. In prayers of intercession, some people fold their **hands** while others open them, palms up.

When we were baptized, the **sign of the cross** was traced on our foreheads. In some Christian communions, the cross is traced on the lips and the heart as well. Since the earliest centuries, Christians have traced the cross on their foreheads or their bodies when they rise in the morning, at prayer, and when they go to bed at night. With this simple gesture women, men, and children are marked for life at baptism.

Parents may bless their children just as friends may bless each other by placing their two **hands on the head** of the other person. It is an intimate gesture as old as Abraham and as new as the mother who places her hands on the head of her young child. Such a gesture conveys favor, affection, and love.

Some people **kneel** as they pray, others **stand** or **sit**. Some people pray while walking, running, or working. The simple gestures of everyday life—open arms in welcome, an embrace, a handshake, washing, planting, eating—can be the gestures of prayer. The more momentous transitions of life—birth, leaving home, entering school, moving and separation, marriage, sickness, birthdays and reunions, dying and death—can be the opportunities for household prayer. May *Welcome Home* assist you in the daily, Sunday, and seasonal rhythm of prayer.

The Gospel of Mark

Through the course of this year almost all of the Gospel of Mark will be read. That fact gives the attentive reader an occasion to extend his or her knowledge of the book that most scholars consider to be the first "gospel" written.

Yet, much more than Mark is read in this year. John appears in great strength, and Matthew and Luke make appearances at important festivals. Large passages of at least six different New Testament letters are read in sequence. And a significant passage of the Hebrew Scriptures sets the tone of the lections, again and again, as the First Reading for nearly every Sunday and festival. To call this all "the year of Mark" might be to miss the astonishing force, the symbolic power, even the *mystery* with which this combination of readings is endowed.

This "Second Gospel" (to use its old but misleading title) can indeed be seen as establishing the character of the lectionary of the year, even when its own text is not read. Even a casual reader of Mark notes certain striking things. For one, the accounts of Jesus' activity are constantly surrounded by misunderstanding, even on the part of his closest disciples. Jesus' own mother and brothers think he is mad (Mark 3:21, 31). For another, Jesus himself is continually charging those around him to keep silent regarding his power and his identity. The mystery only grows upon a closer reading: Jesus' identity is plainly recognized only by unclean spirits (1:24-25) or by one of the soldiers who killed him (15:39). There is profound misunderstanding (8:27-33) or mocking rejection (15:25-32). And Jesus' teaching seems *intended* to cloak and hide and puzzle, with only a *promise* of final open revelation (4:11-12, 21-22).

Trained by the story we know from the other Gospels, we then expect these puzzles to be resolved by the resurrection, by the story of the disciples' encounter with the risen Jesus. Here again, Mark confounds us. When we reach the end of the book (16:8, according to the best witnesses), there has been no resurrection appearance, only the promise to see him in Galilee, "just as he told you," followed by fear and flight and silence. The attentive reader will then begin to read the book again, perhaps initially in frustration. With the help of the believing community, it may then slowly dawn on the reader that there are other persons besides demons and murderers who know the true identity of Jesus: The community that is reading the Gospel knows! It has been revealed to them from the very first verse (1:1)! Demons, murderers and we ourselves (for we, too, are among the unclean) know this: Jesus is Messiah or Christ or "Son of God" in ways utterly unexpected of a saving king. He is among the unclean; he suffers; he dies. Even more: The community discovers that beginning in 1:16 they are in Galilee again. And, just as he said, they *see him*.

Then it is clear. *The reading of book itself is the resurrection appearance.* Such reading is now the open proclamation of the mystery (4:21-23). When we read the Gospel, we are enacting a faith that is already present in Mark's Gospel. Martin Luther was right to propose that when we read of Christ coming and going, healing and helping, we should understand that he is coming here, bringing us to himself, carrying us, healing us. But the Christ whom we see in the reading of this book is always a surprising one, calling for faith to trust that he is indeed God's Christ. He is a king who rules by littleness and dying; he is God where some people think God cannot be, among the sinners and the impure; and so he is the resurrection and salvation of all things. But then every text in Mark is to be read with the story of Jesus' passion and death in mind, and every text is to be read next to 16:1-8. Every text is thereby made into a bearer of the saving presence of God.

The Gospel of John, for example, seems to intend exactly the same purpose with its readings. The Fourth Gospel moves through a series of "signs" such as John 2:11 and "discourses" such as 6:25-71, all the while waiting for the crucial "hour" of Jesus (see 2:4), which these things signify and toward which they point. That hour comes (13:1), and when it comes it brings Jesus' death and resurrection as loving service, as salvation, as the very presence of God (13:20). The community is invited to meet on Sunday, the day of resurrection, to encounter the wounds of the Risen One in faith and to be sent as witnesses. And every story of Jesus is written to enable that encounter in faith, that coming to life (20:31). To read a passage of John, thus, is always to be brought face to face with Jesus' "hour," with his death and resurrection, the gift of the Spirit, and the possibility of faith.

If the lectionary readings are meant to proclaim the presence of the crucified and risen Christ to us now, if they are meant to carry us—as Luther says—in the arms of Christ, under the power of the Spirit, into the very presence of God, then their meaning will be clearer as these particular readings lead the household of faith to the Sunday gathering: to the table of the the word, to the baptismal font, and to the holy supper. How do these texts, these biblical readings, wash us into God and clothe us in Christ? How do we "eat and drink" the presence of Christ in reading them? Both Mark and John make clear that these questions are not strange to their intentions.

For what is written in the lectionary is written that we might believe—lay down upon, be carried by, be clothed in, be bathed in, be held by, eat and drink—this: that Jesus is the Christ, the Son of God, and that believing we may have life in his name (John 20:31).

Daily

*I*n a society caught up in the demanding rhythm of schedules and the ever-present voice of radio and television, daily prayer is an essential reality for those who seek to hear God's voice and cultivate an inner life. Whether one prays alone or with others, in simplicity or festive delight, with brevity or sustained meditation, the rhythm of daily prayer reveals the life-sustaining communion to which God invites all human beings. Such prayer is a serene power silently at work, drawing us into the ancient yet vital sources of faith, hope, and love.

Since the earliest days of Christianity, the followers of Jesus have prayed as he did: in the morning, in the evening, and before going to bed. When possible they have prayed, though briefly, at midday. This rhythm of prayer follows the daily cycle—sunrise, noon, sunset, nighttime—and allows the Christian community to recognize the living presence of Christ in all times and all places: upon waking to a new day, during the rush of labor, in the darkness of night. "If I ascend to heaven, you are there," writes the psalmist, "if I make my bed in Sheol, you are there. If I take the wings of morning and settle at the farthest limits of the sea, even there your hand shall lead me, and your right hand shall hold me fast" (Psalm 139:8-11).

Our prayer may be the simple invocation of Christ's name or the blessing of the Trinity, repeated throughout the day. It may include the reading of a psalm or a selection of scripture. We may pray the Lord's Prayer—the model of all Christian prayer—three times a day. When members of a

Prayer

household gather for a meal, both the simple and festive patterns of prayer outlined in *Welcome Home* may be shared among those present.

While Christians gather on the Lord's day—Sunday—for public worship, much of our time is spent in the home. We first learn the words, the gestures, and the songs of faith in the home. We discover our essential identity as a community of faith in the home. We mark the many significant transitions of life—from birth to death—in the home. To surround and infuse the daily rhythm of sleeping and waking, working and resting, bathing and eating with the words and gestures of Christian prayer is to discover the ancient truth of the gospel: the ordinary and the human can reveal the mystery of God and divine grace.

Like planets around the sun, our daily prayer draws us to the Sunday assembly where we gather for the word and the breaking of the bread in the seasons of the year. From the Sunday assembly, our daily prayer flows into the week.

> Christ be with me, Christ within me,
>   Christ behind me, Christ before me,
> Christ beside me, Christ to win me,
>   Christ to comfort and restore me.
> Christ beneath me, Christ above me,
>   Christ in quiet, Christ in danger,
> Christ in hearts of all that love me,
>   Christ in mouth of friend and stranger.
>
> *St. Patrick's Breastplate*

Daily Prayer

UPON WAKING

Upon waking, trace a small cross on the lips and say,

O Lord, open my lips,
and my mouth will declare your praise

or

The Sacred Three be over me,
the blessing of the Trinity.

FOR EVERY DAY

I rise before dawn and cry for help;
    I put my hope in your words.
My eyes are awake before each watch of the night,
    that I may meditate on your promise. *Psalm 119:147-148*

Awake, my soul!
Awake, O harp and lyre!
    I will awake the dawn.
I will give thanks to you, O Lord, among the peoples;
    I will sing praises to you among the nations.
For your steadfast love is as high as the heavens;
    your faithfulness extends to the clouds. *Psalm 57:8-10*

O Light of light and sun of day,
come shine on us your brightest ray.
    Ambrose of Milan

I bind unto myself today
    the strong name of the Trinity
by invocation of the same,
    the Three in One and One in Three.
    St. Patrick's Breastplate

I give thanks to you, my heavenly Father,
through Jesus Christ your dear Son,
that you have protected me through the night
from all harm and danger
and I ask that you also protect me today from sin
    and every danger,
so that my life and actions may please you.
Into your hands I commend my body, my soul,
    and all that is mine.
Let your holy angel be with me,
so that the wicked foe may have no power over me. Amen.
    Luther's morning prayer

FOR THE LORD'S DAY

Holy Spirit,
dawn upon this soul of mine,
glow within this heart of mine,
fortify this will of mine,
still this restless heart of mine,
wake my spirit,
clear my sight,
purge me with your holy fire.
    Samuel Longfellow

Help, save, comfort, and defend us, gracious Lord.
    Kyrie

This is the feast of victory for our God. Alleluia.
    Worthy is Christ, the Lamb who was slain,
        whose blood set us free to be people of God.
    Hymn of Praise from the Revelation to John

Holy God, mighty Lord, gracious Father:
    Endless is your mercy and eternal your reign.
You have filled all creation with light and life;
    heaven and earth are full of your glory.
    Eucharistic Prayer I

Prayer in the Morning

INVITATION

Trace a small cross on the lips and say,
O Lord, open my lips,
and my mouth will declare your praise.
Psalm 51:15

HYMN

Awake, O sleeper, rise from death,
and Christ shall give you light;
so learn his love, its length and breadth,
its fullness, depth, and height.

To us on earth he came to bring
from sin and fear release,
to give the Spirit's unity,
the very bond of peace.

Then walk in love as Christ has loved,
who died that he might save;
with kind and gentle hearts forgive
as God in Christ forgave.

For us Christ lived, for us he died,
and conquered in the strife.
Awake, arise, go forth in faith,
and Christ shall give you life.
Tune: AZMON (Oh, for a thousand tongues to sing)

PSALM 63:2-9

God, my God, you I crave;
my soul thirsts for you,
my body aches for you
like a dry and weary land.
Let me gaze on you in your temple:
a vision of strength and glory.

Your love is better than life,
my speech is full of praise.

I give you a lifetime of worship,
my hands raised in your name.
I feast at a rich table,
my lips sing of your glory.

On my bed I lie awake,
your memory fills the night.
You have been my help,
I rejoice beneath your wings.
Yes, I cling to you,
your right hand holds me fast. [ICEL]

SCRIPTURE

A passage from scripture or a reading from the daily lectionary may be read here, followed by silence.

THE SONG OF ZECHARIAH

Blessed are you, Lord, the God of Israel,
you have come to your people and set them free.
You have raised up for us a mighty Savior,
born of the house of your servant David.
Through your holy prophets, you promised of old
    to save us from our enemies,
    from the hands of all who hate us,
    to show mercy to our forebears,
    and to remember your holy covenant.
This was the oath you swore to our father Abraham:
    to set us free from the hands of our enemies,
    free to worship you without fear,
    holy and righteous before you,
    all the days of our life.

And you, child, shall be called the prophet of the Most High,
for you will go before the Lord to prepare the way,
to give God's people knowledge of salvation
by the forgiveness of their sins.
In the tender compassion of our God
the dawn from on high shall break upon us,
to shine on those who dwell in darkness and the shadow of death,
and to guide our feet into the way of peace.
    Benedictus, Luke 1:68-79

PRAYERS

Prayer for others and ourselves
The Lord's Prayer

O Lord, almighty and everlasting God,
you have brought us in safety to this new day;
preserve us with your mighty power,
that we may not fall into sin, nor be overcome in adversity;
and in all we do, direct us to the fulfilling of your purpose;
through Jesus Christ our Lord.
Amen

BLESSING

May the God of hope fill us with all joy and peace
through the power of the Holy Spirit. Amen
See Romans 15:13

At Midday

INVITATION

> Whatever you do, in word or deed,
> do everything in the name of the Lord Jesus.
> *Colossians 3:17*

PSALM 113

> Hallelujah!

> Servants of God, praise,
> praise the name of the Lord.
> Bless the Lord's name
> now and always.
> Praise the Lord's name
> here and in every place,
> from east to west.

> The Lord towers above nations,
> God's glory shines over the heavens.
> Who compares to our God?
> Who is enthroned so high?

> The Lord bends down
> to see heaven and earth,
> to raise the weak from the dust
> and lift the poor from the mire,
> to seat them with princes
> in the company of their leaders.

> The childless, no longer alone,
> rejoice now in many children.

> Hallelujah! [ICEL]

SCRIPTURE

We know love by this, that he laid down his life for us—and we ought to lay down our lives for one another. How does God's love abide in anyone who has the world's goods and sees a brother or sister in need and yet refuses help? Little children, let us love, not in word or speech, but in truth and action.

1 John 3:16-18

PRAYERS

Prayers for others and ourselves
The Lord's Prayer

Blessed Savior,
at this hour you hung upon the cross,
stretching out your loving arms:
Grant that all the peoples of the earth
may look to you and be saved;
for your tender mercies' sake.
Amen

BLESSING

The LORD preserve us from all evil;
Keep us safe and watch our going and coming,
now and forever. Amen

See Psalm 121:7-8

Prayer in the Evening

INVITATION

Make the sign of the cross and say,
O God, come to my assistance.
O Lord, hasten to help me.
See Psalm 70:1

HYMN

Light of undying glory, shine,
warming our hearts with love divine;
come from the gracious Father's side,
bathe us in joy this eventide.

Lord Jesus Christ, your living breath
restores the world from sin and death;
giver of life and Lord of grace,
show us the splendor of your face.

Westward the sun is lost to sight,
the star of ev'ning marks the night;
be, Lord, the lamp that sheds the glow
of heaven's radiance here below.

All-holy Father, only Son,
Spirit of love, forever one,
let all the world its voice now raise
to sing your everlasting praise.
Tune: O WALY WALY *(When love is found) or* TALLIS' CANON

PSALM 141:1-5, 8-10

Hurry, Lord! I call and call!
Listen! I plead with you.
Let my prayer rise like incense,
my upraised hands, like an evening sacrifice.

Lord, guard my lips,
watch my every word.
Let me never speak evil
or consider hateful deeds,
let me never join the wicked
to eat their lavish meals.

If the just correct me,
I take their rebuke as kindness,
but the unction of the wicked
will never touch my head.
I pray and pray
against their hateful ways.

Lord my God, I turn to you,
in you I find safety.
Do not strip me of life.
Do not spring on me
the traps of the wicked.
Let evildoers get tangled
in their own nets,
but let me escape. [ICEL]

SCRIPTURE

*A passage from scripture or a reading from the daily lectionary may be
read here, followed by silence.*

THE SONG OF MARY

My soul proclaims the greatness of the Lord,
my spirit rejoices in God my Savior,
for you, Lord, have looked with favor on your lowly servant.
From this day all generations will call me blessed:
> you, the Almighty, have done great things for me
> and holy is your name.
> You have mercy on those who fear you,
> from generation to generation.
You have shown strength with your arm
and scattered the proud in their conceit,
casting down the mighty from their thrones
and lifting up the lowly.
You have filled the hungry with good things
and sent the rich away empty.
You have come to the aid of your servant Israel,
to remember the promise of mercy,
the promise made to our forebears,
to Abraham and his children for ever.
Magnificat, Luke 1:46-55

PRAYERS

Prayers for others and ourselves
The Lord's Prayer

God our creator,
abide with us as evening comes.
Calm our souls,
refresh our bodies,
keep us close to Christ
and draw us to one another.
Be with us and with all people
until the morning light appears.
Amen

BLESSING

May the peace of God,
which surpasses all understanding,
guard our hearts and minds in Christ Jesus.
See Philippians 4:7

At Bedtime

INVITATION

When going to bed, make the sign of the cross and say,
The Lord almighty grant us a quiet night
and peace at the last.

PSALM 139:1-12

You search me, Lord, and know me.
Wherever I sit or stand,
you read my inmost thoughts;
whenever I walk or rest,
you know where I have been.

Before a word slips from my tongue,
Lord, you know what I will say.
You close in on me,
pressing your hand upon me.
All this overwhelms me—
too much to understand!

Where can I hide from you?
How can I escape your presence?
I scale the heavens, you are there!
I plunge to the depths, you are there!

If I fly toward the dawn,
or settle across the sea,
even there you take hold of me,
your right hand directs me.

If I think night will hide me
and darkness give me cover,
I find darkness is not dark.
For your night shines like day,
darkness and light are one. [ICEL]

SCRIPTURE

I am convinced that neither death, nor life, nor angels, nor rulers, nor things present, nor things to come, nor powers, nor height, nor depth, nor anything else in all creation, will be able to separate us from the love of God in Christ Jesus our Lord.

Romans 8:38-39

RESPONSE

Into your hands, O Lord, I commend my spirit.
You have redeemed me, O Lord, God of truth.
Into your hands I commend my spirit.

THE SONG OF SIMEON

Guide us waking, O Lord,
and guard us sleeping;
that awake we may watch with Christ
and asleep we may rest in peace.

Now, Lord, you let your servant go in peace:
your word has been fulfilled.
My own eyes have seen the salvation
which you have prepared in the sight of every people:
a light to reveal you to the nations
and the glory of your people Israel.

Nunc dimittis, Luke 2:29-32

PRAYERS

Prayers for others and ourselves
The Lord's Prayer

Visit this house,
we beg you, Lord,
and banish from it
the deadly power of the evil one.
May your holy angels dwell here
to keep us in peace,
and may your blessing be always upon us.
We ask this through Christ our Lord.
Amen

or

I give thanks to you, my heavenly Father,
through Jesus Christ your dear Son,
that you have graciously protected me today,
and I ask you to forgive me all my sins, where I have done wrong,
and graciously to protect me tonight.
For into your hands I commend myself:
my body, my soul, and all that is mine.
Let your holy angel be with me,
so that the wicked foe may have no power over me.
Amen
    Luther's evening prayer

Bedtime Prayer with Children

SONGS

Go, my children, with my blessing, never alone;
waking, sleeping, I am with you, you are my own;
in my love's baptismal river I have made you mine forever,
go, my children, with my blessing, you are my own.
Tune: AR HYD Y NOS (God, who made the earth and heaven)

Children of the heav'nly Father
safely in his bosom gather;
nestling bird nor star in heaven
such a refuge ne'er was given.

Though he giveth or he taketh,
God his children ne'er forsaketh;
his the loving purpose solely
to preserve them pure and holy.
Tune: TRYGGARE KAN INGEN VARA, Swedish folk tune

Refrain:
All night, all day, angels watching over me, my Lord.
All night, all day, angels watching over me.

Now I lay my down to sleep.
Angels watching over me, my Lord.
Pray the Lord my soul to keep.
Angels watching over me. *Refrain*

Lord, stay with me through the night.
Angels watching over me, my Lord.
Wake me with the morning light.
Angels watching over me. *Refrain*

Sun of my soul, O Savior dear,
it is not night if you are near;
Oh, may no earthborn cloud arise,
to hide you from your servant's eyes.

Come near and bless us when we wake,
as through the world our way we take,
Till through your love which knows no end
we gain at last the peace of heaven.

Tune: TALLIS' CANON *(All praise to you, my God, this night)*

Thy holy wings, O Savior, spread gently over me
and let me rest securely through good and ill in thee.
Oh, be my strength and portion, my rock and hiding place,
and let my ev'ry moment be lived within thy grace.

Oh, wash me in the waters of Noah's cleansing flood.
Give me a willing spirit, a heart both clean and good.
Oh, take into thy keeping thy children great and small,
and while we sweetly slumber, enfold us one and all.

Tune: BRED DINA VIDA VINGAR, *Swedish folk tune,*
or AURELIA *(The Church's one foundation)*

PRAYERS

The LORD is my shepherd, I shall not want.
Psalm 23:1

The LORD is my light and my salvation;
whom shall I fear?
Psalm 27:1

Stay with us, Lord.
Luke 24:29

Lord, you know that I love you.
John 21:16

Come, Lord Jesus, and night shall be no more.
See Revelation 21:5

Angel sent by God to guide me,
be my light and walk beside me;
be my guardian and protect me;
on the paths of life direct me.

Now I lay me down to sleep,
I pray the Lord my soul to keep.
He is the branch and I am the flower,
May God send me a happy hour.

The King of love my shepherd is,
whose goodness faileth never;
I nothing lack if I am his
and he is mine forever.

BLESSINGS

May the LORD bless us and keep us,
both now and forever. Amen

The LORD is your keeper;
the LORD is your shade at your right hand.
The sun shall not strike you by day,
nor the moon by night.
Psalm 121:5-6

May the God of love and peace be with you.
2 Corinthians 13:11

God is love,
and those who abide in love abide in God,
and God abides in them.
1 John 4:16

Receive the cross of Christ.

Let your light shine before others.

Peace be with you.

Sunday

*F*rom the earliest days of our history, Christians have called Sunday "the Lord's day," the first day of the week when God created light. Ancient Christians called the day of Christ's resurrection "the eighth day," a new day on which God brought life and light out of death and darkness. As scripture attests, Christ appears to his followers on Sunday, the first day of the week. He gathers them through the power of the Spirit, he explains the scriptures and breaks bread, he offers his gift of peace, and sends his disciples forth to continue his mission in the world. Sunday remains for Christians the day on which we celebrate our immersion in his life through baptism and our sustenance in that life through the supper. Sunday marks the public gathering of Christians and the renewal of their mission in the rhythm of daily life.

Christians celebrate the Lord's day from the setting of the sun on Saturday evening until nightfall on Sunday. We mark this day from sunset to sunset in various ways: with prayer, song, reading from the scriptures, renewing our baptism, and joining other Christians for worship. We may celebrate the day of resurrection with a simple invocation of Christ's name or a festive meal surrounded with lights, prayers, and songs. While we gather with the baptized on the Lord's day for the celebration of the word and meal, we also recognize that the risen Christ appears in the many ordinary places of life: in houses and apartments, in a garden and by a lake, in the sharing of a meal, and walking with friends on a road

(Luke 24; John 20–21). Celebrating Sunday in the home brings to greater awareness the presence of Christ among us and with us in our daily tasks and gatherings.

The celebration of Sunday may begin simply with a prayer to Christ the Light. On festive occasions, use a greater selection of songs, psalms, and readings. It is always appropriate to offer thanksgiving for baptism on the day of resurrection. As night falls, light a candle and pray or sing to Christ the Light, read a selection from scripture, or simply repeat a short verse of scripture. Let this day end in the peace of Christ.

Sunday Morning

INVITATION

Make the sign of the cross and say,
This is the feast of victory for our God. Alleluia.

HYMN

On this day, the first of days,
God the maker's name we praise;
who, creation's Lord and spring,
did the world from darkness bring.

On this day the eternal Son
over death his triumph won;
on this day the Spirit came
with its gifts of living flame.

God, the blessed Three in One,
may your holy will be done;
In your word our souls are free,
as we praise the Trinity.
> Tune: *NUN KOMM, DER HEIDEN HEILAND* (*Savior of the nations, come*)
> or *PATMOS* (*Take my life, that I may be*)

PSALM 118:24-29

This is the day the Lord made,
let us rejoice and be glad.
Lord, give us the victory!
Lord, grant us success!

Blest is the one who comes,
who comes in the name of the Lord.
We bless you from the Lord's house.
The Lord God is our light:
adorn the altar with branches.

I will thank you, my God,
I will praise you highly.
Give thanks, the Lord is good,
God's love is for ever! [ICEL]

SCRIPTURE

A passage from scripture or a reading from the daily lectionary may be read here, followed by silence.

CANTICLE

The Song of Zechariah (page 21) or

We praise you, O God,
we acclaim you as Lord;
all creation worships you,
the Father everlasting.
To you all angels, all the powers of heaven,
the cherubim and seraphim, sing in endless praise:
    Holy, holy, holy Lord, God of power and might,
    heaven and earth are full of your glory.
The glorious company of apostles praise you.
The noble fellowship of prophets praise you.
The white-robed army of martyrs praise you.
Throughout the world the holy Church acclaims you:
    Father, of majesty unbounded,
    your true and only Son, worthy of all praise,
    the Holy Spirit, advocate and guide.

You, Christ, are the king of glory,
the eternal Son of the Father.
When you took our flesh to set us free
you humbly chose the Virgin's womb.
You overcame the sting of death
and opened the kingdom of heaven to all believers.
You are seated at God's right hand in glory
We believe that you will come to be our judge.
    Come then, Lord, and help your people,
    bought with the price of your own blood,
    and bring us with your saints
    to glory everlasting.
    Te Deum

PRAYERS

Prayers for others and ourselves
The Lord's Prayer

In the beginning, O God,
you created light on this day
and gave to all creation a sign of your favor.
On this day, your mighty hand
raised Christ from the darkness of death
and filled all creation with the light of life.
Your Spirit calls us to praise you for this day,
a foretaste of the last and great day
when the shadows and darkness of death will be no more.
Come to us, we pray,
and be our light, our word, and our food,
until we see you in our eternal home.
Amen

BLESSING

May God who has given us a new birth into a living hope
through the death and resurrection of Jesus Christ,
bless us and keep us now and forever.
Amen
See 1 Peter 1:3

THANKSGIVING FOR BAPTISM

If used, this prayer may take place around a bowl of water
with a lighted candle.

Holy God, mighty Lord,
we give you thanks
for you nourish and sustain us and all living things
with the gift of water.
In the beginning your Spirit moved over the waters
and you created heaven and earth.
By the waters of the flood you saved Noah and his family.
You led Israel through the sea out of slavery into the promised land.
In the waters of the Jordan
your Son was baptized by John and anointed with the Spirit.

By the baptism of his death and resurrection
your Son set us free from sin and death
and opened the way to everlasting life.

We give you thanks, O God,
that you have given us new life in the water of baptism.
Buried with Christ in his death,
you raise us to share in his resurrection by the power of the Holy
    Spirit.
May all who have passed through the water of baptism
continue in the risen life of our Savior.

To you be all honor and glory, now and forever.
Amen

*Each person may dip a hand into the water and make the sign of the cross in
remembrance of his or her baptism.*

SUNDAY MEAL PRAYER

As we gather at this table,
we offer you thanks, O God,
for the gifts of food and drink
that you have given us for our enjoyment.
As we share this meal on the day of resurrection,
strengthen us to serve the risen Christ in word and deed.
Enlighten us with your grace
so that we may help those who hunger and thirst for light and life.
We ask this through Christ our Lord.
Amen

Sunday Evening

INVITATION

Light one candle and say,
Jesus Christ is the light of the world,
the light no darkness can overcome.

THANKSGIVING FOR LIGHT

We bless you, O Lord our God,
creator of the universe,
who led your people Israel with a pillar of cloud by day
and a pillar of fire by night.
Make our darkness bright with the light of Christ
and keep us safe until the the coming of your dawn
when all creation will praise the light that never fades.
To you be all glory, O God,
Father, Son, and Holy Spirit,
now and forever.
Amen

HYMN

Abide with me, fast falls the eventide.
The darkness deepens; Lord, with me abide.
When other helpers fail and comforts flee,
Help of the helpless, oh, abide with me.

I need thy presence ev'ry passing hour;
what but thy grace can foil the tempter's pow'r?
Who like thyself my guide and stay can be?
Through cloud and sunshine, oh, abide with me.

I fear no foe, with thee at hand to bless;
ills have no weight, and tears no bitterness.
Where is death's sting? Where, grave, thy victory?
I triumph still, if thou abide with me!
Tune: EVENTIDE

PSALM 67

Favor and bless us, Lord.
Let your face shine on us,
revealing your way to all peoples,
salvation the world over.

Let nations sing your praise,
every nation on earth.

The world will shout for joy,
for you rule the planet with justice.
In fairness you govern the nations
and guide the peoples of earth.

Let the nations sing your praise,
every nation on earth.

The land delivers its harvest,
God, our God, has blessed us.
O God, continue your blessing,
may the whole world worship you. [ICEL]

SCRIPTURE

*A passage from scripture or a reading from the daily lectionary may be
read here, followed by silence.*

CANTICLE

The Song of Mary (page 27) or

Let the same mind be in you
that was in Christ Jesus,
who, though he was in the form of God,
did not regard equality with God
as something to be exploited,
but emptied himself, taking the form of a slave,
being born in human likeness.

And being found in human form,
he humbled himself
and became obedient to the point of death—
even death on a cross.

Therefore God also highly exalted him
and gave him the name that is above every name,
so that at the name of Jesus
every knee should bend,
in heaven and on earth and under the earth,
and every tongue should confess
that Jesus Christ is Lord,
to the glory of God the Father.
Philippians 2:5-11

PRAYERS

Prayers for others and ourselves
The Lord's Prayer

Lord God,
whose Son our Savior Jesus Christ triumphed over the powers of
    death
and prepared for us our place in the new Jerusalem:
Grant that we, who have this day given thanks for the resurrection,
may praise you in that City of which he is the light,
where he lives and reigns with you and the Holy Spirit,
one God now and for ever.
Amen

BLESSING

May the grace of our Lord Jesus Christ be with us all.

The Prayers of Christians

KYRIE

Lord, have mercy.
Christ, have mercy.
Lord, have mercy.

GLORIA PATRI

Glory to the Father, and to the Son,
and to the Holy Spirit:
as it was in the beginning, is now,
and will be for ever. Amen.

APOSTLES' CREED

I believe in God, the Father almighty,
creator of heaven and earth.

I believe in Jesus Christ, God's only Son, our Lord,
who was conceived by the Holy Spirit,
born of the Virgin Mary,
suffered under Pontius Pilate,
was crucified, died, and was buried;
he descended to the dead.
On the third day he rose again;
he ascended into heaven,
he is seated at the right hand of the Father,
and he will come to judge the living and the dead.

I believe in the Holy Spirit,
the holy catholic Church,
the communion of saints,
the forgiveness of sins,
the resurrection of the body,
and the life everlasting. Amen.

SANCTUS

Holy, holy, holy Lord, God of power and might,
heaven and earth are full of your glory.
　　Hosanna in the highest.

Blessed is he who comes in the name of the Lord.
　　Hosanna in the highest.

THE LORD'S PRAYER

Our Father in heaven,
　　hallowed be your name,
　　your kingdom come,
　　your will be done,
　　　　on earth as in heaven.
Give us today our daily bread.
Forgive us our sins
　　as we forgive those who sin against us.
Save us from the time of trial
　　and deliver us from evil.

For the kingdom, the power, and the glory are yours
　　now and for ever. Amen.

LAMB OF GOD

Lamb of God, you take away the sin of the world,
　　have mercy on us.
Lamb of God, you take away the sin of the world,
　　have mercy on us.
Lamb of God, you take away the sin of the world,
　　grant us peace.

Advent

*A*dvent is like a stump. The growing season is over, the crops have been harvested and the fields are bare. All over North America trees and bushes are down to their brown branches, with most of the leaves and all the colorful flowers and fruits gone. In caves and burrows throughout the continent animals are hibernating. Dusk comes earlier every day, as if the daylight is being cut off before our eyes. People sit under sunlamps to treat their depression, because the darkness has them feeling like stumps themselves.

But a stump still has its roots. There is always the possibility that its root system will send up fresh sprigs and a new tree will grow in the old place. A hibernating bear is not dead, just waiting out the cold, and we can be sure that the bear will emerge, yawning and stretching and hunting again as soon as the weather warms up. Even though the deciduous trees seem, as Charles Dickens said of Jacob Marley, "dead as a doornail," there is every hope that in some weeks or months green buds will appear.

The lectionary readings for Advent are about our being a stump and yet hoping for new life. We read ancient poems of a subjugated people whose glorious monarchy had been destroyed. Their poets write of their life as a faded leaf, of themselves as withered grass. Yet they are hopeful that a time of blessing will come. They recall that King David was promised an everlasting reign, and they are confident that a new king will be born: God will respond to their deep yearning for blessing, justice, and peace. Yes, people are hungry and tables are bare. But there is the hope that bounty will appear, for a stump does have roots that can sprout anytime. John the Baptist, half-mad with indignation at the desert he sees in people's lives, promises that something is coming to stir life into dried branches.

Thus Advent is like the winter landscape, appearing bleak and barren, but pregnant with promise. Thus, of course, Advent is like each one of us at sometime in our life. Our joys cut down, we feel as if we are a piece of wood that other people are sitting on top of. It seems as if nothing in or around us is still alive. Maybe it is unemployment: will a job ever come through? Maybe we await word from the physicians: will life be worth living if my beloved is dead? One doesn't get through life without these dry and deathly times.

But we hope. The roots are still reaching into the soil. We continue trusting that tomorrow, or next week, or next spring, the situation will improve. When I personally am close to despair, my friends and family and neighbors hope for me, reminding me of the promise of new life.

Advent is a time for the Christian community to practice hope. We acknowledge that we are stumps, but that God has promised us new growth. So we huddle together in the dark and chill, awaiting the life of God. Even if our roots are dead, we trust that God's grace will awaken our life and send out new shoots. We remind one another to stay awake in case the dawn comes and we miss it. We keep each other company as we anticipate the arrival of the angel, announcing the good news.

North American Advent fits well the season of the

earth—the natural calendar—since the year itself is at its stump. But what is particularly dissonant is that Advent is totally out of sync with the North American secular calendar. The secular calendar turns all of December, and increasing November as well, into a Saturnalia, a month of revels, a continuous party to end the old year and bring in the new. For many people the month is utterly exhausting, with shopping and decorating and baking and concerts and drinking and wrapping. Yet this orgy of celebration is called by the name of Christ, and it is carols about Jesus' birth piped into the malls on December 1 that stimulate us to spend more money. By December 26, Christmas is gone, and Valentine cards appear.

The church need not be an Ebenezer Scrooge, grumping about secular Christmas, badmouthing the fun. Cultures commonly celebrate at the winter solstice. But maintaining Advent has profound human benefit, and the church dismisses or truncates this liturgical season to its own loss. Human beings need to acknowledge the stumpiness of life. We all go through times of great need, and, finally, death. If you're doing just fine now, then look around, because others, who need what you have, aren't. We all need to pratice hope, to try it out for some weeks each year, so that when misery comes, and it will, we know how to call it up in ourselves and within the community. How will we know where hope is, if we never planted it, cultivated it, watered it?

Some Christians do little to observe the liturgical year. At the time of the Reformation, some Protestants abandoned the church year, judging it an unnecessary constraint from church authorities. For several centuries in North America, Christianity spread on the prairie with few resident churches or clergy, and in people's kitchens the liturigcal year languished. What resulted was that all these human emotions had to be experienced individually: *I* had to experience guilt by myself; *I* alone had to seek the word of life; *I* had to get ecstatic, if I was the personality-type to get ecstatic, when the Spirit entered me. In religious matters, the individual was isolated from others.

The liturgical year allows a season each year for us all to accompany one another through life. We practice these feelings each year, and best of all, we practice them together. Yes, we are all stumps, you this year, I next, but I also a stump this year because of you. And we all hope for God's life. Come on, you're not dead yet! We'll make it together. Have you heard the news? The wilderness is crowded with people splashing in the river, Mary is pregnant with a new King David, and here are bread and wine, the beginning of the feast.

An increasing number of churches decorate themselves for Advent with blue. Sometimes the color is a deep blue, the sky just before sunrise; sometimes it is a lighter tone, the color of a springtime bird's egg. While the culture inundates the surroundings with Christmas trees and lights and red bows, Advent asks us to keep practicing hope. Remember the poor; stand with the unemployed; visit the mourners. If you dress the virgin Mary in a blue gown, remember that she was not serenely smiling through a normal pregnancy. No: she was hoping, for a husband who would not abandon her, for money to pay the tax, for a place to give birth, for the world to receive whatever was about to spring forth.

Praying in Advent

INVITATION

The King shall come when morning dawns
and light triumphant breaks.

TABLE PRAYER

As we prepare for the advent of your Son, O God,
we give you thanks for this food and drink,
signs of your gracious love.
May this meal strengthen us to share your gifts
with the hungry and all who look for your justice and mercy.
Grant this through Christ our Lord.
Amen

HYMN

O Lord, how shall I meet you, how welcome you aright?
Your people long to greet you, my hope, my heart's delight!
Oh, kindle, Lord most holy, your lamp within my breast
to do in spirit lowly all that may please you best.

Your Zion strews before you green boughs and fairest palms;
and I, too, will adore you with joyous songs and psalms.
My heart shall bloom forever for you with praises new
and from your name shall never withhold the honor due.

Love caused your incarnation; love brought you down to me.
Your thirst for my salvation procured my liberty.
Oh, love beyond all telling, that led you to embrace
in love, all love excelling, our lost and fallen race.

Tune: VALET WILL ICH DIR GEBEN (All glory, laud, and honor)

PSALM 85

Lord, you loved your land,
brought Jacob back,
forgot our guilt,
forgave our sins,
swallowed your anger,
your blazing anger.

Bring us back,
saving God.
End your wrath.
Will it stop,
or drag on for ever?

Turn, revive us,
nourish our joy.
Show us mercy,
save us, Lord!

I listen to God speaking:
"I, the Lord, speak peace,
peace to my faithful people
who turn their hearts to me."
Salvation is coming near,
glory is filling our land.

Love and fidelity embrace,
peace and justice kiss.
Fidelity sprouts from the earth,
justice leans down from heaven.

The Lord pours out riches,
our land springs to life.
Justice clears God's path,
justice points the way. [ICEL]

SCRIPTURE

See the daily readings

CANTICLE

In the morning, the Song of Zechariah (page 21)
In the evening, the Song of Mary (page 27)
At bedtime, the Song of Simeon (page 29) or

The wilderness and the dry land shall be glad,
    the desert shall rejoice and blossom;
like the crocus it shall blossom abundantly,
    and rejoice with joy and singing.

The glory of Lebanon shall be given to it,
    the majesty of Carmel and Sharon.
They shall see the glory of the Lord,
    the majesty of our God.

Then the eyes of the blind shall be opened,
    and the ears of the deaf unstopped;
then the lame shall leap like a deer,
    and the tongue of the speechless sing for joy.
For waters shall break forth in the wilderness,
    and streams in the desert.

And the ransomed of the Lord shall return,
    and come to Zion with singing;
everlasting joy shall be upon their heads;
    they shall obtain joy and gladness,
    and sorrow and sighing shall flee away.
        Isaiah 35:1-2, 5-6, 10

PRAYER

Prayers for others and ourselves
The Lord's Prayer

God of love and faithfulness,
you so loved the world
that you gave your only Son to be our Savior.
Help us to receive him as our Lord and brother
and freely celebrate his advent among us
as our redeemer now and forever.
Amen

BLESSING OF THE HOUSEHOLD BIBLE

With the beginning of the liturgical year in Advent, the church hears a new set of readings from scripture. Use this blessing at the beginning of Advent or whenever the scriptures are read.

Eternal Wisdom,
we offer you thanks for the Word of God,
our Lord and Savior Jesus Christ.
As we read and ponder the scriptures,
open our eyes so that we may recognize him
and help us hear his voice
so that we may know your will and grow in every good work.
We ask this through Christ our Lord.
Amen

BLESSING OF THE ADVENT WREATH

*The lighting of the wreath may begin Advent prayer in the home.
Use this blessing throughout Advent as a new candle is lighted each Sunday.*

Lord our God,
you call all people to walk in your light
and to seek your justice and peace.
Bless us as we light the candle(s) of this wreath.
Strengthen us in hope
that we may be ready to greet our Lord when he comes
and welcome him into our hearts and homes.
We make this prayer in the name of him
who is our light and our salvation.
Amen

THE O-ANTIPHONS

During the final week of Advent, an O-Antiphon is sung each day, usually in the evening before the Song of Mary.

December 17

O come, O Wisdom from on high, who governs all things tenderly;
to us the path of knowledge show, and teach us in her ways to go.
> *Refrain:*
> *Rejoice! Rejoice! Emmanuel shall come to you, O Israel.*

December 18

O come, O come, great Lord of might,
who to your tribes on Sinai's height
in ancient times once gave the law
in cloud, and majesty, and awe. *Refrain*

December 19

O come, O Flower of Jesse's Root,
before whom all the world stands mute.
We trust your mighty power to save,
and give us victory o'er the grave. *Refrain*

December 20

O come, O Key of David, come,
and open wide our heavenly home;
make safe the way that leads on high,
and close the path to misery. *Refrain*

December 21

O come, O Dayspring, come with cheer;
O Sun of Justice, now draw near.
Disperse the gloomy clouds of night,
and death's dark shadow put to flight. *Refrain*

December 22

O come, O Keystone,
come and bind in one the hearts of humankind.
Come bid our sad divisions cease,
and be for us the King of peace. *Refrain*

December 23

O come, O come, Emmanuel, and ransom captive Israel,
that mourns in lonely exile here until the Son of God appear.
> *Refrain*

Daily Readings and Prayers

First Sunday of Advent

S	Isa. 64:1-9		Ps. 80:1-7, 17-19
	I Cor. 1:3-9		Mark 13:24-37
M	Zech. 13:1-9	**T**	Zech. 14:1-9
W	Matt. 24:16-35	**Th**	Micah 2:1-13
F	I Thess. 4:13-18	**S**	Ps. 80

For prayer throughout the day

> Let your face shine on us, O Lord, and we shall be saved.
> *See Psalm 80:3*

A prayer for the week

> Lord Jesus,
> we do not lack any spiritual gift as we wait for your coming.
> Keep us awake and help us use our gifts
> to serve those who look for the dawn of your justice and mercy.
> Amen

Second Sunday of Advent

S	Isa. 40:1-11		Ps. 85:1-2, 8-13
	2 Peter 3:8-15a		Mark 1:1-8
M	Isa. 6:1-13	**T**	Isa. 1:1-17
W	Mark 11:27-33	**Th**	Mal. 2:17—3:4
F	Acts 11:1-18	**S**	Ps. 85

For prayer throughout the day

> Prepare the way of the Lord. *Mark 1:3*

A prayer for the week

> God our shepherd,
> gather us as lambs in your arms.
> Forgive our sins so that we may rejoice in your coming.
> Amen

Third Sunday of Advent

S	Isa. 61:1-4, 8-11		Ps. 126
	1 Thess. 5:16-24		John 1:6-8, 19-28
M	Mal. 4:1-5	**T**	Deut. 18:15-22
W	Mark 9:9-13	**Th**	2 Kings 2:9-22
F	Acts 3:17—4:4	**S**	Ps. 125

For prayer throughout the day

The Lord has anointed me to bring good news to the oppressed.
Isaiah 61:1

A prayer for the week

Lord Jesus, you continue to do great things for us.
Give us your gift of peace as we await your coming.
Amen

Fourth Sunday of Advent

S	2 Sam. 7:1-11, 16		Luke 1:47-55
	Rom. 16:25-27		Luke 1:26-38
M	1 Sam. 1:1-28	**T**	1 Sam. 2:1-11
W	Luke 1:67-79	**Th**	Judges 13:2-25
F	Rom. 16:1-20	**S**	Ps. 89:1-37

For prayer throughout the day

I am your servant. Help me live according to your word.
See Luke 1:38

A prayer for the week

God our Savior,
nothing is impossible for you.
Prepare our hearts to rejoice in your glorious advent.
Amen

Christmas

*A*t Christmas, all the trees of the wood are singing for joy. Spruces, pines, cedars, and firs liven up the short daylight with their many shades of green. In front yards and town squares evergreens are strung with hundreds of lights, and countless homes and stores, offices and church buildings have brought trees indoors and decorated them up with paper stars, colored balls, lights, and ribbons. If we could find a moment of quiet on Christmas Day, we could hear all these trees singing.

The solstice has come and gone. On or about December 21, the earth turned and now each day brings us several more minutes of light. In ancient times this was a period filled with great celebrations: all would not die; the sun has been reborn; decorate the cold bleak houses with evergreens and light the candles. The increasing darkness in the Northern Hemisphere had been reversed: light is alive after all. And because light was restored, it seemed that the evergreen trees were singing that we all would survive.

Thus it was that the fourth-century Christians recognized the similarity between the solstice, the return of natural light, and the nativity of the Lord—the coming of God's light in human form. It was as if the winter solstice provided the perfect metaphor for the incarnation. The world is a dark place, growing darker and darker. Any thoughtful person questions whether the end is approaching. But in the birth of Jesus, God enters the dying world. Death turns around. The light shines, and the darkness cannot overcome it. And so on Christmas Day, Christians pray the psalm in which all the trees of the wood are singing for joy.

On Christmas Eve, when we read from Luke's Gospel, the Prayer of the Day praises the light come into the dark night. On Christmas Day we read the beginning of John's Gospel, in which what is born among us at Christmas is the very light with which God created the world. John's "In the beginning" echoes Genesis 1, for the annual winter solstice reminds us of both the first creation of the world and of its re-creation in Christ. And here is an interesting note: the prayer for Christmas Day is the same prayer appointed for the First Reading at the Easter Vigil. So we are reminded that the light of the incarnation, which is the light of creation, is also the light of Christ bursting forth brilliantly at the resurrection.

Even to a people who understand the movement of the planets around the sun, the solstice is a wonderful gift. Like a surprise, the increasing light makes us smile. The trees are singing with the promise that spring will come. Christmas is a time of joyous surprise, as we receive God's gifts of life yet again. The darkness has not overwhelmed us. And yet the gift of Christ comes to us together: the bread and wine, the body and blood of Christ, are given *for you*, that is, for *all* of you. In a simple, almost hidden way, we receive God's gift of life.

The joy of this subtle surprise contrasts with the dominant mood of letdown that North American culture experiences during the Twelve Days of Christmas. Crisis centers report these days to be a time of great family turmoil, of most suicide attempts, of deepest personal loneliness. Santa Claus promised us perpetual happiness, a mythic family gathering, mounds of toys, all of our heart's desires. But we must admit it didn't happen. Heaven didn't establish itself in the living room this year.

Christian Christmas is different from secular Christmas. Christian Christmas begins, rather than concludes, on the evening of December 24. It lasts twelve days, rather than twelve hours. It celebrates the light of Christ in a world that remains in most ways exceedingly dark. It seeks to discover the gift that God is, rather than being disappointed that God or someone else didn't come through with the gift we wanted. Christian Christmas is the beginning of joy, not the end of it. Secular Christmas suggests that a roly-poly man drops down from the sky to give us everything on our list. Of course we are disappointed. Christian Christmas gives us the life of the Trinity: the Creator of light, Christ our light, and the shining Spirit, the God who means to make of us the light that the dark world seeks.

We see the difference between secular Christmas and Christian Christmas in the saints' observances that fall in the Twelve Days. While everyone lines up at the mall to return rejected Christmas presents, the church observes the life and death of Stephen, the first martyr; John, the writer whose visionary poem of the birth of light connects the nativity with the creation of the first light; the Holy Innocents, the boy babies of Bethlehem killed out of King Herod's fear; and the Name of Jesus, the day to remember that in the incarnation God becomes an embodied person just like one of us. With the saints we sing the angelic song, "Glory to God in the highest," and with the martyrs we pray, "Receive our prayer."

Because secular Christmas is for so many people a

painful time, a season of disappointment and loneliness, it is important for the church's Christmas to be other. Let it be among us a time of telling the truth in love. Let it be a time for sharing in the gift of Christ's body and blood. Let us remind one another that, all evidence to the contrary notwithstanding, God is born among us and light has come. Let us receive the gift, and be gift to one another. And let us walk away from the piped-in music long enough to hear all the trees of the wood singing for joy.

Praying in Christmas

INVITATION

The Word became flesh and lived among us,
and we have seen his glory.
John 1:14

TABLE PRAYER

With shepherds and angels, we sing:
Glory to God in the highest
and peace to God's people on earth.
With Mary and Joseph we praise you, O God,
for Christ, the Word made flesh.
With joyful hearts we offer you thanks
for the gifts that grace this table.
Strengthen us with this food,
that we may be witnesses to the light shining in darkness.
We ask this in the name of our Savior, Christ the Lord.
Amen

HYMN

Oh, come, all ye faithful, joyful and triumphant!
Oh, come ye, oh, come ye to Bethlehem;
come and behold him born the king of angels:
Refrain:
Oh, come, let us adore him, oh, come, let us adore him,
oh, come, let us adore him, Christ the Lord!

The highest, most holy, Light of light eternal,
born of a virgin, a mortal he comes;
Son of the Father now in flesh appearing! *Refrain*

Sing, choirs of angels, sing in exultation,
sing, all ye citizens of heaven above!
Glory to God in the highest: *Refrain*

PSALM 96:7-13

> Proclaim the Lord, you nations,
> praise the glory of God's power,
> praise the glory of God's name!
> Bring gifts to the temple,
> bow down, all the earth,
> tremble in God's holy presence.
>
> Tell the nations, "The Lord rules!"
> As the firm earth is not swayed,
> nothing can sway God's judgment.
> Let heaven and earth be glad,
> the sea and sea creatures roar,
> the field and its beasts exult.
>
> Then let the trees of the forest sing
> before the coming of the Lord,
> who comes to judge the nations,
> to set the earth aright,
> restoring the world to order. [ICEL]

SCRIPTURE

See the daily readings

CANTICLE

In the morning, the Song of Zechariah (page 21)
In the evening, the Song of Mary (page 27)
At bedtime, the Song of Simeon (page 29) or

Glory to God in the highest,
and peace to God's people on earth.

Lord God, heavenly King,
almighty God and Father
    we worship you, we give you thanks,
    we praise you for your glory.

Lord Jesus Christ, only Son of the Father,
Lord God, Lamb of God,
you take away the sin of the world:
    have mercy on us;
you are seated at the right hand of the Father:
    receive our prayer.

For you alone are the Holy One,
you alone are the Lord,
you alone are the Most High,
    Jesus Christ,
    with the Holy Spirit,
    in the glory of God the Father. Amen.
        Gloria in excelsis Deo, Luke 2:14 with acclamations

PRAYER

Prayers for others and ourselves
The Lord's Prayer

Almighty God,
you have filled us with the new light
of the Word who became flesh and lived among us.
Let the light of our faith shine in all that we do;
through your Son, Jesus Christ our Lord,
who lives and reigns with you and the Holy Spirit,
one God, now and forever.
Amen

BLESSING OF THE CHRISTMAS TREE

Use this blessing when you first light the tree and whenever you gather for Christmas prayer by the tree.

God our creator,
we praise you for this Christmas tree,
gift of the earth and sign of your evergreen presence.
As we illumine this tree,
let your blessing come upon us.
Send us your Son,
the tender branch of Jesse,
who brings us light and life.
May we who stand in its light
eagerly welcome the true Light which never fades.
All glory be yours now and forever.
Amen

BLESSING OF GIFTS

Use this blessing before you open gifts.

Blessed be your name, O God,
you are the source of every blessing.
From your hand we receive the good gifts
of life, health, and salvation.
As we give and receive these presents,
bless us with hearts thankful for the gift of your Son
and lead us to share from our abundance with the poor and needy.
We ask this through Christ our Lord.
Amen

BLESSING OF THE NATIVITY SCENE

Use this blessing when figures are added to the nativity scene throughout the days of Christmas and on the Epiphany.

O Lord our God,
with Mary and Joseph,
angels and shepherds,
and the animals in the stable,
we gather around your Son, born for us.
Bless us with your holy presence
and inspire us to help those who have no place to dwell.
Be with us that we might share Christ's love with all the world,
for he is our light and salvation.
Glory in heaven and peace on earth,
now and forever.
Amen

BLESSING FOR THE NEW YEAR

Use this blessing on New Year's Eve or New Year's Day

O God,
you have been our help in ages past,
our hope for years to come.
As we welcome this new year,
bless us with peace.
Fill our days with light of Christ
and lead us on the path of life
until we see you in our heavenly home.
You live and reign forever and ever.
Amen

Daily Readings and Prayers

Christmas Day

Dec. 25	Isa. 52:7-10		Ps. 98
	Heb. 1:1-4		John 1:1-14
Dec. 26	Luke 2:1-20	**Dec. 27**	Isa. 62:6-12
Dec. 28	Ps. 96	**Dec. 29**	Gen. 1:1—2:4a
Dec. 30	Ps. 97	**Dec. 31**	Heb. 1:1-12
Jan. 1	Num. 6:22-27		Ps. 8
	Gal. 4:4-7		Luke 2:15-21

For prayer throughout the day

    Glory to God, and peace to all people on earth. *See Luke 2:14*

A prayer for the days after Christmas

    Lord God,

    may your Word become flesh through our lives

    so that we may see him in the fullness of his glory.

    Amen

First Sunday after Christmas

S	Isa. 61:10—62:3		Ps. 148
	Gal. 4:4-7		Luke 2:22-40
M	Lev. 12:1-8	**T**	Exod. 13:11-16
W	Mark 8:27—9:1	**Th**	Isa. 49:5-12
F	Acts 13:42-52	**S**	Ps. 145

For prayer throughout the day

    My eyes have seen your salvation. *Luke 2:31*

A prayer for the week

    God our Father,

    we are no longer orphans but children of yours in Jesus Christ.

    May we come to greater wisdom through your Word made flesh.

    Amen

Second Sunday after Christmas

S Jer. 31:7-14   Ps. 147:12-20
      Eph. 1:3-14   John 1:10-18

For prayer throughout the day

Let us live for the praise of God's glory. *See Ephesians 1:12*

A prayer for the week

Word made flesh,
we have received of your fullness, grace upon grace.
Give us wisdom to live in your light
and serve those who dwell in the shadows and darkness of death.
Amen

Epiphany

*D*epending on where you live in North America, this may happen to you during January and February once, or many times: when you go to bed at night, all the trees and bushes are naked brown, bare branches and stalks, but in the morning every single twig is overlaid with glistening ice. Each evergreen needle is wearing a stunning cloak of ice. A drab scene has been transformed into another world, a fairyland; one may even expect to see tiny beautiful creatures dancing on the branches. How can such small twigs hold so much ice? How can our yard, which appeared so dead, be so miraculously transfigured? But look quickly, right now: the sun will soon melt all the shimmering magic away. Perhaps as the sun begins its shining, we will glimpse minute rainbows on some of the branches.

The icy cover changes how we live. Some of us are glad to walk slowly, to creep the car carefully along, for we want time to see the spectacular sight. The ice, which is nothing more than quite cold water, has realigned everything.

Each Gospel narrative in the Epiphany season is like another ice storm, transforming the scene with amazing water and with shimmering light. The season begins with the Magi traveling across the miles and presenting royal gifts to a newborn. Mary and Jospeh look outside and are astonished to see on their doorstep an entourage of sages—surely more than three, probably wise women as well—altering their lives. In the sky is a star so brilliant that one can follow its movement. The season moves from the Magi honoring an infant to the disciples witnessing the transfiguration. In both stories only a few people are alert enough to see the transformation that Christ has brought to the world.

The infant grows up and is baptized by John, and the heavens open and a dove descends, the sky itself has broken open. Early Christians said that on that surprising day all the waters of the earth were renewed and all the monsters who lurked in the seas were defeated. Some fishermen recognize something new and abandon their nets. The crowd sees only Jesus of Nazareth, but a madman glimpses the glory of God manifested before him, and the evil demon escapes as quickly as it can. Those bound by fever, leprosy, and paralysis see a bright light shining in Christ, and their restraints melt away. God is revealed, and all is new.

Like the ice that melts by midmorning, these transformations do not radiate a perpetual glow hour after hour, day after day. You have to be in the right place at the right time to see them. You have to help one another remember them, and be there again next week to glimpse them again, trusting in the dark and barren time that such enlightenment is possible once more. Yes, there was that dazzling vision of the glorious Christ meeting with Moses and Elijah, two visionaries who had actually seen God; but too quickly the scene is over, and we see only an ordinary person standing there alone. Our baptisms are over, and it seems like the same persons there, the same hungry baby, the same adults with their problems still there. Baptism affords no continous halo. We wear albs for an hour, but then we take them off, and for the rest of the week Christians seem to be simply ordinary people.

And what is going on outside during the weeks of Epiphany? The wind is cold, sometimes bitter. People who describe life on the prairie say that the weather is trying to kill you. It is dark, and people stay indoors. Nothing much happens these weeks. Concerts are cancelled. City folk, who pretend that their buildings will keep them safe, complain at having to wear mufflers and mittens, or they freeze because they refuse to. Valentines wallpaper the stores in red, trying to liven things up. On February 15 the red hearts disappear, and pastel Easter bunnies begin hopping around the mall, spreading through these nastiest weeks of the year their pagan hope that springtime will come.

In great contrast, the church calls this time Epiphany and practices enlightenment. Together we glimpse a glory of God that others are not seeing. It is the season to admit that God's splendor is not like that of a Hollywood production, all enthusiastic action to amuse the viewer. Rather, Epiphany is gathering each week on bleak Sundays because we have faith that God will diamond-coat the trees. The demon within us will flee before the shining light, and at least for an hour we will see in each other's faces a kind of luminous spirit.

Epiphany is a good time for catechesis. North America has long had the pattern that with the fields too frozen for cultivation, winter was the time for education. School went on when farming didn't. But whether we work in the fields or go to the lake during the summer, we can spend these winter weeks in study of and service to the light of Christ. Perhaps we can examine all the light imagery in the liturgy, or sing all the Epiphany and morning hymns, or a have a discussion on where we see God's light illumining our dark world. It is a good time to sit together in a warm room and help one another see.

Don't forget, however, to keep one eye to the window. There is frost on the panes, the field is wearing a bright, white alb, and the branches donned a silver cope overnight.

Praying in Epiphany

INVITATION

Arise, shine; for your light has come,
and the glory of the LORD has risen upon you.
Isaiah 60:1

TABLE PRAYER

O good and gracious God,
we praise you for the light of Christ
that shines in our midst.
Receive our thanks for the gifts of this table
and strengthen us with your love
that we may be light
for those who dwell in darkness and the shadows of death.
Grant this through Christ our Lord.
Amen

HYMN

Songs of thankfulness and praise, Jesus, Lord, to thee we raise;
manifested by the star to the sages from afar,
Branch of royal David's stem in thy birth at Bethlehem:
Anthems be to thee addressed, God in flesh made manifest.

Manifest at Jordan's stream, Prophet, Priest, and King supreme;
and at Cana wedding guest in thy Godhead manifest;
manifest in pow'r divine, changing water into wine:
Anthems be to thee addressed, God in flesh made manifest.

Grant us grace to see thee, Lord, present in thy holy Word;
grace to imitate thee now and be pure, as pure art thou;
that we might become like thee at thy great epiphany,
and may praise thee, ever blest, God in flesh made manifest.
Tune: SALZBURG
or ST. GEORGE'S, WINDSOR (Come, you thankful people, come)

PSALM 72:1-8

God, give your king judgment,
the son of the king
your sense of what is right;
help him judge your people
and do right for the powerless.

May mountains bear peace,
hills bring forth justice.
May the king defend the poor,
set their children free,
and kill their oppressors.

May he live as long as the sun,
as long as the moon, for ever.
May he be like rain on a field,
like showers that soak the earth.

May justice sprout in his time,
peace till the moon is no more.
May he rule from sea to sea,
from the River to the ends of the earth. [ICEL]

SCRIPTURE

See the daily readings

CANTICLE

In the morning, the Song of Zechariah (page 21)
In the evening, the Song of Mary (page 27)
At bedtime, the Song of Simeon (page 29) or

The spirit of the Lord GOD is upon me,
    because the LORD has anointed me;
he has sent me to bring good news to the oppressed,
    to bind up the brokenhearted,
to proclaim liberty to the captives,
    and release to the prisoners;
to proclaim the year of the LORD's favor,
    and the day of vengeance of our God;
    to comfort all who mourn;
to provide for those who mourn in Zion—
    to give them a garland instead of ashes,
the oil of gladness instead of mourning,
    the mantle of praise instead of a faint spirit.
They will be called oaks of righteousness,
    the planting of the LORD, to display his glory.

I will greatly rejoice in the LORD,
    my whole being shall exult in my God;
for he has clothed me with the garments of salvation,
    he has covered me with the robe of righteousness,
as a bridegroom decks himself with a garland,
    and as a bride adorns herself with her jewels.

For as the earth brings forth its shoots,
    and as a garden causes what is sown in it to spring up,
so the Lord GOD will cause righteousness and praise
    to spring up before all the nations.
        Isaiah 61:1-3, 10-11

PRAYER

Prayers for others and ourselves
The Lord's Prayer

Lord God,
on this day you revealed your Son to the nations
by the leading of a star.
Lead us now by faith to know your presence in our lives,
and bring us at last to the full vision of your glory,
through your Son, Jesus Christ our Lord,
who lives and reigns with you and the Holy Spirit,
one God, now and forever.
Amen

Almighty God,
you sent your Son to proclaim your kingdom
in word and deed.
Anoint us with the power of your Spirit,
that we may bring good news to the afflicted,
bind up the brokenhearted,
and proclaim liberty to the captive;
through your Son, Jesus Christ our Lord.
Amen

THANKSGIVING FOR BAPTISM

Use this prayer on the Baptism of the Lord or throughout the days
of Epiphany

O Christ,
the light of a star led the Magi to you.
Help us guide others to your unfading light.

O Christ,
in the River Jordan you were proclaimed God's beloved child.
Strengthen us in our baptism as your brothers and sisters.

O Christ,
you have brought us through the waters of death to new life.
Renew in us the power of your Spirit
so that we may follow you in peace.

O Christ,
you were anointed by the Spirit to bring good news to the afflicted.
Give us the grace to serve all those in need.

PRAYERS FOR THE UNITY OF CHRISTIANS

*Use these texts during the Week of Prayer for Christian Unity, the third week
in January*

As you, Father, are in me
and I am in you,
may they also be in us,
so that the world may believe that you have sent me.
The glory that you have given me
I have given them,
so that they may be one, as we are one.
John 17:21-22

Gracious Father,
we pray for your holy catholic Church.
Fill it with your truth.
Keep it in your peace.
Where it is corrupt, reform it.
Where it is in error, correct it.
Where it is right, defend it.
Where it is in want, provide for it.
Where it is divided, reunite it;
for the sake of your Son, our Savior Jesus Christ.
Amen

Daily Readings and Prayers

Epiphany of the Lord

Jan. 6	Isa. 60:1-6		Ps. 72:1-7, 10-14
	Eph. 3:1-12		Matt. 2:1-12
Jan. 7	Exod. 1:8-22	**Jan. 8**	Exod. 2:1-10
Jan. 9	Mark 2:13-21	**Jan. 10**	Zeph. 3:8-11
Jan. 11	Eph. 2:11-22	**Jan. 12**	Ps. 72

For prayer throughout the day

We have seen his star; come, let us adore him. *See Matthew 2:2*

A prayer for the week

God of light,
the glory of the Lord has risen upon us.
May the gifts we share with those in need
be signs of our love for you.
Amen

Baptism of the Lord

S	Gen. 1:1-5		Ps. 29
	Acts 19:1-7		Mark 1:4-11
M	Gen. 6:11-22	**T**	Gen. 8:1-19
W	John 1:28-34	**Th**	Isa. 41:14-20
F	Acts 22:2-16	**S**	Jonah 2:1-10

For prayer throughout the day

May we, your beloved ones, be pleasing to you. *See Mark 1:11*

A prayer for the week

Creator God,
you separated light from darkness.
Send us your Spirit so that we may live
as beloved sons and daughters of the light.
Amen

Second Sunday after the Epiphany

S   I Sam. 3:1-10   Ps. 139:1-6, 13-18
       I Cor. 6:12-20   John 1:43-51
M   I Sam. 11:5-15   **T**   I Sam. 15:10-31
W   Luke 3:23-38   **Th** Gen. 29:10-22
F   2 Cor. 6:11—7:1   **S**   Ps. 89:1-37

For prayer throughout the day

    Lord, you know all my ways. Lay your hand upon me.
       See Psalm 139:3, 5

A prayer for the week

    Lord Jesus,
    you have invited us to come and see the mystery of your kingdom.
    Form us daily into the temple of the Spirit,
    for we have been saved with a great price.
    Amen

Third Sunday after the Epiphany

S   Jonah 3:1-5, 10   Ps. 62:5-12
       I Cor. 7:29-31   Mark 1:14-20
M   Gen. 12:1-9   **T**   Gen. 45:25—46:7
W   Mark 3:13-19   **Th** Prov. 8:1-21
F   I Cor. 7:1-31   **S**   Ps. 62

For prayer throughout the day

    Let me live the good news of salvation. *See Mark 1:15*

A prayer for the week

    Lord Jesus, our rock and our salvation,
    you called your disciples to follow you for the sake of others.
    Give us courage to use the power you bestow on us
    for the good of those in need.
    Amen

Fourth Sunday after the Epiphany

S	Deut. 18:15-20		Ps. 111
	1 Cor. 8:1-13		Mark 1:21-28
M	Jer. 23:30-40	**T**	Jer. 29:1-14
W	Mark 5:1-20	**Th**	Isa. 41:14-20
F	1 Cor. 7:32-40	**S**	Ps. 13

For prayer throughout the day

Jesus is the Lord through whom I live. *See 1 Corinthians 8:6*

A prayer for the week

God our redeemer,

you have shown your graciousness to all who look upon Jesus
Christ.

Strengthen us in our struggle with the powers of evil

that we may be light for the world.

Amen

Fifth Sunday after the Epiphany

S	Isa. 40:21-31		Ps. 147:1-11, 20c
	1 Cor. 9:16-23		Mark 1:29-39
M	2 Kings 4:8-37	**T**	2 Kings 8:1-7
W	Mark 3:7-12	**Th**	Job 6:1-13
F	1 Cor. 9:1-16	**S**	Ps. 147

For prayer throughout the day

The LORD heals the brokenhearted. *Psalm 147:3*

A prayer for the week

Lord Jesus,

be our strength in weakness,

our healing in sickness,

and our gate to eternal life.

Amen

Sixth Sunday after the Epiphany

S	2 Kings 5:1-14		Ps. 30
	I Cor. 9:24-27		Mark 1:40-45
M	Lev. 13:1-17	**T**	Lev. 14:1-32
W	Mark 3:1-6	**Th**	Job 30:16-31
F	I Cor. 10:14—11:1	**S**	Ps. 6

For prayer throughout the day

O LORD, be my helper in time of need. *See Psalm 30:10*

A prayer for the week

In the waters of baptism, O God,

you have washed us clean.

Renew the cleansing power of your grace in our lives.

Amen

Seventh Sunday after the Epiphany

S	Isa. 43:18-25		Ps. 41
	2 Cor. 1:18-22		Mark 2:1-12
M	Isa. 30:18-26	**T**	Micah 4:5-8
W	Mark 8:11-13	**Th**	Job 7:1-21
F	2 Cor. 1:1-11	**S**	Ps. 38

For prayer throughout the day

Be our strength, O God, in times of sickness. *See Psalm 41:3*

A prayer for the week

Lord Jesus,

open our hearts to receive your healing power.

Forgive us our sins, renew our strength,

and lead us to serve all in need.

Amen

Eighth Sunday after the Epiphany

S   Hosea 2:14-20   Ps. 103:1-13, 22
      2 Cor. 3:1-6   Mark 2:13-22
M   Ezek. 16:1-14   **T**   Ezek. 16:53-63
W   John 3:22-36   **Th** Isa. 62:1-5
F   2 Cor. 1:23—2:17 **S**   Ps. 103

For prayer throughout the day
   The LORD is merciful and gracious. *Psalm 103:8*

A prayer for the week
   O Lord,
   you nourish us with your body, the bread of life.
   Lead us to feed the hungry and care for those in need
   for your name's sake.
   Amen

Transfiguration of the Lord

S   2 Kings 2:1-12   Ps. 50:1-6
      2 Cor. 4:3-6   Mark 9:2-9
M   Exod. 19:7-25   **T**   1 Kings 19:9-18

For prayer throughout the day
   God, open my heart to listen to your beloved Son. *See Mark 9:7*

A prayer for the week
   Father of Jesus Christ,
   your glory shines forth through your Son,
   with whom you are well pleased.
   Gather us with all your beloved people
   into the glory you have prepared for us in Jesus Christ.
   Amen

Lent

Spring is beginning. It is time to hike over to the tree of life and cut off a walking stick for the journey ahead.

We hear a lot about journeys these days. With the world changing so fast and each decade pushing us into a new place, many people describe their life as a journey. Nothing stays settled very long, and the metaphor of a journey helps us turn our insecurities into adventures. Whether the distance covered is in miles or kilometers, or whether it is through one's past memories and future fears, we move along as if on a journey, heading—we hope—toward happiness.

Springtime is a good time to start such a journey. The earth itself is beginning a journey from drab brown to multi-colored flowers, from bitter winds to balmy days. The weather calls us to join it in a journey towards life. In many places the snow is melting, and we need the water as much as the earth does. In other places, the chill is evaporating as more humid winds begin to swirl.

Perhaps because of our culture's increasing urbanization and technology, many people begin in springtime to plan actual journeys: summer treks, backpacking hikes, vacations away, to find adventure or contentment or the self. Some people hope that on their next journey they will find their heart's desire, while some use their journey to escape the search altogether. Many North Americans spend thousands of dollars to purchase equipment with which to pretend that they have merged with nature. Many people have come to believe that life is better or deeper somewhere else. But even as the bags are packed, we know that these journeys promise far more than they can ever deliver.

Springtime is then an annual return of the perpetual human search for life. We are tired of winter. Let us move to a better frame of mind. Let us go deeper. Yes, people crave stability, and many people find too much movement upsetting, even chaotic. But the opposite is also true: people do not want to stagnate. They want to be growing. They want to know that they are on the move.

The word in Old English for springtime was "lencten," from which we get our word *Lent*. Indeed, the season of Lent fits surprisingly well in the springtime of the Northern Hemisphere, for Lent is the time for Christians to embark on a unique journey. We have seen the glory of Christ on the mountain of transfiguration, and we realize that we must begin the journey together. We need to head out of winter, into the beginning of spring, and up to the mountain of God. We need to be moving toward the flowing water of the streams that God gushes out.

We had better take along a walking stick for our journey. Like Moses with his staff, we can lean on it when life gets strenuous. Perhaps, like Moses' staff, it will swallow up snakes, divide the sea in two, and assure victory during the battle. Perhaps, like a shepherd's crook, it will merely assist us in our daily tasks. But any serious hiker finds a walking stick useful. Two legs and two arms are not always enough. To say it another way, we can use the vertical post of Christ's cross as the best walking stick around.

Thanks to the liturgical year, we do not walk or hike

alone. We have not only our walking sticks; we have each other. Yes, like Elijah, we have forty days to journey to the mountain of God. Yes, like Elijah, we often moan and groan: I am the only one left. But just as God chided Elijah, so God must chuckle at us: "Look around! There are thousands with you." We are not merely tramping about, roaming here and there. We walk together in company, sometimes striding, sometimes plodding, but always marching up to Zion. Lent is the time when all the baptized journey together from winter to spring, from death of life, from dirt and thirst to the renewing waters. The triune God journeys with us, having traveled already from heaven to earth, from the manger to the cross, from Jesus into the community.

We begin the journey on Ash Wednesday. Many Christians adopt a forty-day practice to mark the journey. They eat less, or give away more, or pray longer, or limit their entertainment, to help them stay focused on the goal. Pilgrims travel light. We join Jesus in the wilderness for forty days, battling our demons. But thanks to Christ, we are not alone, as he was. We have one another for comfort and our walking sticks for support. In fact, those walking sticks sometimes come in handy as cudgels, good strong staffs to beat the demons away, a cross to conquer the enemy.

We hear during Lent the story from Numbers of the fiery serpents. There we are, all of us journeying together, away from slavery, toward the promised land, and we find ourselves dying from poisonous snakes. But in our midst, on a great walking stick, Moses places a bronze serpent. Together we pray, and together we are healed. But not only the little disgusting snakes must die: according to the words of Christ, we ourselves must die. We must let the old skin sluff off before we can slide into the waters of life. We are a seed that must die before we can bear fruit.

In an earlier time, the church often preached that the faithful had to endure sufferings until God brought relief in heaven. Perhaps in a world where people had very little control over the conditions of their lives, this was sage advice. But now Christians are suggesting something else: that the baptized life is a journey toward liberation, that we are to travel together away from oppression and suffering, helping one another arrive together at the feast. Scholars describe religion as serving two opposite functions: it provides security and it inspires change. Lent is the forty days for change, for leaving the old and walking together toward the new. So pick up your staff, and come.

Praying in Lent

INVITATION

Create in me a clean heart, O God,
and put a new and right spirit within me. *Psalm 51:10*

TABLE PRAYER

Lord Jesus Christ,
as you call us to the Lenten fast,
open our hearts to serve our sisters and brothers
who are hungry and in need.
Grace our table with your presence
and strengthen us as we prepare to celebrate the Easter feast.
You live and reign for ever.
Amen

HYMN

Restore in us, O God, the splendor of your love;
renew your image in our hearts, and all our sins remove.

O Spirit, wake in us the wonder of your power;
from fruitless fear unfurl our lives like springtime bud and flower.

Bring us, O Christ, to share the fullness of your joy;
baptize us in the risen life that death cannot destroy.

Three personed God, fulfill the promise of your grace,
that we, when all our searching ends, may see you face to face.
Tune: POTSDAM *(How good, Lord, to be here)*
or SOUTHWELL *(Lord Jesus, think on me)*

PSALM 130

From the depths I call to you,
Lord, hear my cry.
Catch the sound of my voice
raised up, pleading.

If you record our sins,
Lord, who could survive?
But because you forgive
we stand in awe.

I trust in God's word,
I trust in the Lord.
More than sentries for dawn
I watch for the Lord.

More than sentries for dawn
let Israel watch.
The Lord will bring mercy
and grant full pardon.
The Lord will free Israel
from all its sins. [ICEL]

SCRIPTURE

See the daily readings

CANTICLE

In the morning, the Song of Zechariah (page 21)
In the evening, the Song of Mary (page 27)
At bedtime, the Song of Simeon (page 29) or

Christ suffered for us
leaving us an example,
that we might walk
in his footsteps.

He did nothing wrong;
no false word
ever passed his lips.

When they cursed him
he returned no curse.

Tortured, he made no threats
but trusted in the perfect judge.

He carried our sins
in his body
to the cross,
that we might die to sin
and live for justice.
When he was wounded,
we were healed.
1 Peter 2:21-24 [ICEL]

PRAYER

Prayers for others and ourselves
The Lord's Prayer

Merciful God,
each year you give us this joyful season
when we prepare to celebrate
the death and resurrection of the Lord Jesus.
As we keep the holy discipline of these days
turn our prayer into a greater thirst for you,
let our fasting become our service to the hungry,
and grant us a spirit of willing service to those in need.
Renew in us the grace of baptism
so that we might set our hearts on the world
that will never end.
We ask this in the name of your Son,
who lives and reigns with you and the Holy Spirit,
one God, now and for ever.
Amen

BLESSING FOR ASH WEDNESDAY

Use this prayer on Ash Wednesday and during the days of Lent.

Blessed are you, O God of mercy and compassion.
Though we are but dust and ashes,
in baptism we die and rise with Christ.
As we ponder our sin and frailty,
assure us of your forgiveness and grace.
Nourish and sustain us on our Lenten journey,
that marked with the sign of the cross,
we may be brought to the promised land of Easter.
We make this prayer in the name of Jesus
who is Lord for ever and ever.
Amen

THANKSGIVING FOR THE CROSS

*Use this blessing at a place for prayer with a cross
or image of the crucified Lord.*

God our creator,
in the death of your Son,
you reveal your love for the whole creation.
Sealed with the sign of the cross,
you have claimed us as your children in holy baptism.
In these Forty Days,
lead us in our journey by the light of the holy cross
until we come to the joy of Easter's Fifty Days.
Grant this through Christ our Lord.
Amen

BLESSING OF PALMS

Use this blessing when placing palms in the home
after the Palm Sunday liturgy.

God of our salvation,
blessed is the one who comes in the name of the Lord.
Let this palm branch be for us a sign of Christ's victory
and our participation in the saving events of this great and holy
   week.
In our suffering give us faith and courage,
that dying and rising with Christ,
we may enter into the fullness of his glory.
Amen

Daily Readings and Prayers

Ash Wednesday

	Joel 2:1-2, 12-17		Ps. 51:1-17
	2 Cor. 5:20b—6:10		Matt. 6:1-6, 16-21
Th	Dan. 9:1-19	F	Dan. 9:20-27
S	Ps. 5		

For prayer throughout the day

O God, put a new spirit within me. *Psalm 51:10*

A prayer for the week

Merciful God,

you do not despise sinners, but call us to repentance.

Wash us anew in the great waters of your mercy

and feed us on the bread of forgiveness.

Amen

First Sunday in Lent

S	Gen. 9:8-17		Ps. 25:1-10
	I Peter 3:18-22		Mark 1:9-15
M	Job 4:1-21	T	Job 5:1-27
W	Matt. 4:1-11	Th	Prov. 30:1-9
F	I Peter 3:8-17	S	Ps. 25

For prayer throughout the day

Repent, and believe in the good news. *Mark 1:15*

A prayer for the week

Lord Jesus Christ,

in the desert you prepared to proclaim the reign of God.

In these Forty Days, strengthen us to live and proclaim God's
    reign.

Amen

Second Sunday in Lent

S   Gen. 17:1-7, 15-16   Ps. 22:23-31
       Rom. 4:13-25   Mark 8:31-38
M   Gen. 21:1-7   **T**   Gen. 22:1-19
W   Mark 10:32-34   **Th** Jer. 30:12-22
F   Heb. 11:1-19   **S**   Ps. 22

For prayer throughout the day
   Strengthen us to take up our cross and follow you. *See Mark 8:34*

A prayer for the week
   O God,
   you give your people power
   to hope for that which is unseen.
   Strengthen us so that we may follow your Son
   with courage and humility.
   Amen

Third Sunday in Lent

S   Exod. 20:1-17   Ps. 19
       I Cor. 1:18-25   John 2:13-22
M   I Kings 6:1-22   **T**   Ezra 6:1-18
W   Mark 11:15-19   **Th** Jer. 7:1-15
F   I Cor. 3:10-23   **S**   Ps. 132

For prayer throughout the day
   Let the words of my mouth be acceptable to you, O LORD.
         Psalm 19:14

A prayer for the week
   Lord Jesus Christ,
   you are the power and wisdom of God.
   Help us to grow in your wisdom and power
   through the mystery of your dying and rising.
   Amen

Fourth Sunday in Lent

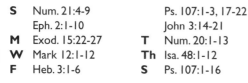

S	Num. 21:4-9		Ps. 107:1-3, 17-22
	Eph. 2:1-10		John 3:14-21
M	Exod. 15:22-27	**T**	Num. 20:1-13
W	Mark 12:1-12	**Th**	Isa. 48:1-12
F	Heb. 3:1-6	**S**	Ps. 107:1-16

For prayer throughout the day

> O God, rich in mercy, make us alive in Christ. *See Ephesians 2:4-5*

A prayer for the week

> Gracious God,
> in your love you gave the world your Son.
> Give us clear vision
> so that we may see your grace and love
> alive in this world and its people.
> Amen

Fifth Sunday in Lent

S	Jer. 31:31-34		Ps. 51:1-12
	Heb. 5:5-10		John 12:20-33
M	Isa. 43:8-13	**T**	Isa. 44:1-8
W	John 12:34-50	**Th**	Hag. 2:1-9
F	2 Cor. 3:4-11	**S**	Ps. 51

For prayer throughout the day

> Jesus, lifted up on the cross, draw your people to salvation.
> *See John 12:32*

A prayer for the week

> God our redeemer,
> your Son came to transform the darkness of human evil into light.
> By the power of his cross and resurrection,
> strengthen us in our struggle against injustice
> and transform us into a merciful people.
> Amen

Holy Week

Passion Sunday

	Isa. 50:4-9a	Ps. 31:9-16
	Phil. 2:5-11	Mark 14:1—15:47
M	Isa. 42:1-9	Ps. 36:5-11
	Heb. 9:11-15	John 12:1-11
T	Isa. 49:1-7	Ps. 71:1-14
	I Cor. 1:18-31	John 21:20-36
W	Isa. 50:4-9a	Ps. 70
	Heb. 12:1-3	John 13:21-32

For prayer throughout the day

Father, not my will but yours be done. *See Mark 14:36*

A prayer for the week

Lord Jesus Christ,
come to us in the power of your Spirit
and prepare our hearts to celebrate the great and holy days.
Amen

Three Days

*A*t first thought, one might choose the cross as the dominant image for the Three Days. But since the Three Days are so paradoxical, a better image might be hyssop.

Hyssop is a shrub that grows between the rocks and around the stone walls that are still, as during biblical times, in Israel. Hyssop is common, humble, with a pleasant aroma, and was used by the ancient Israelites in their religious rituals. On the first Passover, the slaves used a sprig of hyssop to mark their doors with a lamb's blood, so that the angel of death would pass over their houses. The laws of Leviticus stipulate hyssop as an essential ingredient in the cleansing rites of people recovering from disease. Thus hyssop suggests salvation, freedom, and healing. Purge me with hyssop, says Psalm 51, the psalm of David's contrition.

When at the crucifixion Jesus is given sour wine to drink, John's Gospel specifically states that hyssop was used to convey the drink to his mouth. Surely this cannot be a literal reference. Hyssop is not like a sponge, to hold liquid; it does not grow on a long reed, to cover distance. The church has recognized that John's Gospel uses hyssop for a symbolic purpose. The author is teaching us that Christ is the lamb; this is the new passover; the crucifixion is our purification rite; the drink of wine is the new blood to mark our door, that we might be saved.

So let hyssop rest in our imagination these Three Days, the days of Jesus' passover, the Jewish Passover celebration, now the Christian passover. An insigificant scrubby bush is, paradoxically, a hinge between old and new, a clue to the meaning of Jesus' death. It is appropriate to chose a paradoxical image for these days, since paradox—a seeming contradiction that turns out in fact to be true—is the liturgical method of the Three Days.

Many of us were raised with a medieval style Holy Week, a ritual pattern that developed after the fourth century, when Christians visited the Holy Land to try to trace the steps of Jesus' last days. On Palm Sunday, we watched as Jesus entered Jerusalem. On Thursday he ate with his disciples, and on Friday he died. On Saturday we waited, and on Sunday morning we accompanied the women to the empty tomb. On Easter morning, men dress with colorful ties, women wear fancy outfits, the sunshine brightens the banks of spring flowers, the trumpeters are wide awake, and it is easy to believe that life conquers death.

But in recent decades many Christian churches have revived a more ancient Christian observance of these days. The pattern of the first centuries was a much more paradoxical ritual. On Maundy Thursday the church gathers to eat with Christ. The food itself is Christ. Christ, the master, kneels before us to wash our feet, and we, now the body of Christ in the world, kneel before one another to wash each other's feet. On Good Friday we read an ancient poem about a man killed as though he was a lamb slaughtered. We read not Matthew, Mark, or Luke in which Jesus' sufferings are clearly described, but John, in which Christ strides into his passion proclaiming his divinity: "Here I am," he calls out to the arresting soldiers. It is John's Gospel, let us recall, that places hyssop at the cross. We then reverence the cross, and call it good.

The Three Days culminate in the Easter Vigil. Here is paradox at its most complete. We meet in the dark night to praise Christ as the light. We praise the flame of a single candle as if it is brilliantly illuminating the entire room. We read four or seven or twelve stories that tell in paradoxical language the resurrection story: God created the world from chaos; God saved Noah and the animals from the flood; God rescued Isaac from death; God freed the people of Israel from slavery; God serves up a feast for all peoples on the mountain; God rules the world with wisdom and justice; God puts flesh on dry bones; God stands with the three men in the fiery furnace. After these readings with the announcement of the resurrection, we baptize infants as if they were adults, by asking them questions of life-long commitment, and we baptize adults as if they were infants, by washing them again in the womb of the font. We conclude with the eucharistic meal eaten in the middle of the night. One paradox follows another.

The Three Days go on without much help from either nature or the secular culture. Thursday and Friday are regular workdays. Our culture does not halt to eat with Christ, to wash feet, to reverence the cross. True, the malls are filled with pink bunnies and decorated eggs. But these symbols of springtime have more to do with family get-togethers on Sunday afternoon than with the church's gathering in the middle of Saturday night. Despite meeting in the dark, we affirm our faith in the light. Despite dressing warmly for our walk outside, we sing ancient hymns about the birth of spring. Keeping the Great Vigil reminds us that Easter is more than the age-old expectation that chickens will continue to lay eggs and rabbits will keep having litters. Our faith in the resurrection of the body of Christ is more paradoxical than that.

In the Three Days, Christians receive their most concentrated practice of enacting the life of faith. We assemble, perhaps in small numbers, to affirm our faith that in spite of death, we trust in God's life. Most of us need this practice, for we all live through times of mysterious paradox. We all know there are times when a pregnancy met with dread; when death would be a blessing; when our precious children break our hearts; when we must forgive a bitter betrayal; when our choices are despised by others; when we are supposed to sing an Easter hymn at the grave of our beloved. This is life, and life is not easy.

But the God of the Three Days is a surprising, a paradoxical God, a God who lived on earth, rather than safely in heaven; a God who knelt before the faithful people to serve them, rather than the other way around; a God who chose the cross as a throne; a God who overcame death by dying and by enlivening the Christian community. Of course the cross is a sign of the Three Days. But, paradoxically, so is hyssop: a small shrub, a healing plant that signifies life, one way John's Gospel teaches us about the death and life of Christ.

Praying in the Three Days

INVITATION

Let us glory in the cross of our Lord Jesus Christ,
for he is our salvation, our life, and our resurrection.
See Gal. 6:14

TABLE PRAYER

O Christ, the lamb of God,
by your passion, death, and resurrection,
you have brought salvation to the world.
Receive our thankful praise
as we gather at this table,
and nourish us in our paschal journey
from death to eternal life.
You live and reign for ever and ever.
Amen

Maundy Thursday

HYMN

O Jesus, joy of loving hearts,
the fount of life, the light of all:
From ev'ry bliss that earth imparts
we turn, unfilled, to hear your call.

Your truth unchanged has ever stood;
you plead with all to call on you;
to those who seek you, you are good;
to those who find you, life is new.

We taste you, everliving bread,
and long to feast upon you still;
we drink of you, the fountainhead;
our thirsting souls from you we fill.

O Jesus, ever with us stay!
Make all our moments fair and bright!

Oh, chase the night of sin away!
Shed o'er the world your holy light.
> Tune: *WALTON or WOODWORTH (Just as I am)*
> *or ERHALT UNS, HERR (Lord, keep us steadfast in your Word)*

PSALM 116:12-18

What gift can ever repay
God's gift to me?
I raise the cup of freedom
as I call on God's name!
I fulfill my vows to you, Lord,
standing before your assembly.

Lord, you hate to see
your faithful ones die.
I beg you, Lord, hear me:
it is I, the servant you love,
I, the child of your servant.
You freed me from death's grip.

I bring a gift of thanks,
as I call on your name.
I fulfill my vows to you, Lord,
standing before your assembly. [ICEL]

SCRIPTURE

Exod. 12:1-4, 11-14	Ps. 116:1-2, 12-19
1 Cor. 11:23-26	John 13:1-17, 31b-35

CANTICLE

On this mountain the LORD of hosts will make for all peoples
a feast of rich food, a feast of well-aged wines,
of rich food filled with marrow, of well-aged wines strained
clear.
And he will destroy on this mountain
the shroud that is cast over all peoples,
the sheet that is spread over all nations;
he will swallow up death forever.

Then the Lord GOD will wipe away the tears from all faces,
and the disgrace of his people he will take away from all the
earth,
for the LORD has spoken.

It will be said on that day,
Lo, this is our God; we have waited for him, so that he might
save us.
This is the LORD for whom we have waited;
let us be glad and rejoice in his salvation.
Isaiah 25:6-9

PRAYER

Prayers for others and ourselves
The Lord's Prayer

Lord God,
in a wonderful sacrament
you have left us a memorial of your suffering and death.
May this sacrament of your body and blood so work in us
that the way we live will proclaim the redemption you have
brought;
for you live and reign with the Father and the Holy Spirit,
one God, now and forever.
Amen

Good Friday

HYMN

The royal banners forward go;
the cross shines forth in mystic glow
where he, by whom our flesh was made,
in that same flesh our ransom paid;

Where deep for us the spear was dyed,
life's torrent rushing from his side,
to wash us in the precious flood
where flowed the water and the blood.

Fulfilled is all that David told
in true prophetic song of old,
that God the nations' king should be
and reign in triumph from the tree.

To you, eternal Three in One,
our songs shall rise in unison;
those whom you ransom and restore
preserve and govern evermore.
> Tune: TALLIS' CANON
> or ERHALT UNS, HERR (*Lord, keep us steadfast in your Word*)

PSALM 22:2-9, 12-14, 17-20, 23

God, my God,
why have you abandoned me—
far from my cry, my words of pain?
I call by day, you do not answer;
I call by night, but find no rest.

You are the Holy One enthroned,
the Praise of Israel.
Our people trusted, they trusted you;
you rescued them.
To you they cried, and they were saved;
they trusted and were not shamed.

But I am a worm, hardly human,
despised by all, mocked by the crowd.

All who see me jeer at me,
sneer at me, shaking their heads:
"You relied on God; let God help you!
If God loves you, let God save you!"

Do not stay far off,
danger is so close.
I have no other help.
Wild bulls surround me,
bulls of Bashan encircle me,
opening their jaws against me
like roaring, ravening lions.

There are dogs all around me,
a pack of villains corners me.
They tear at my hands and feet,
I can count all my bones.
They stare at me and gloat.
They take what I wore,
they roll dice for my clothes.

Lord, do not stay far off,
you, my strength, be quick to help.
You hear me.

I will proclaim your name to my people,
I will praise you in the assembly. [ICEL]

SCRIPTURE

Isa. 52:13—53:12	Ps. 22
Heb. 10:16-25	John 18:1—19:42

CANTICLE

Let us return to the Lord
who tore us apart
but now will heal us;
who struck us down
yet binds our wounds;
who revives us after two days,
raising us up on the third,
to live in God's presence.

Let us seek to know the Lord,
whose coming is sure as dawn,
who descends like the rain,
spring rain renewing the earth.

For I take delight
not in sacrifices,
but in loyal love;
not in holocausts,
but in the knowledge of God.
Hosea 6:1-3, 6 [ICEL]

PRAYER

Prayers for others and ourselves
The Lord's Prayer

Rejoice, O life-bearing Cross,
the invincible trophy of godliness,
the door of paradise,
the foundation of the faithful,
the protection guarding the church,
by which corruption is utterly destroyed
and the power of death swallowed up
and we are exalted to heaven from earth.
The invincible weapon,
the adversary of demons,
the glory of the martyrs,
the true beauty of saints,
the haven of salvation
which gives great mercy to the world.

By your cross, Lord Jesus,
you have brought life to the world.
Amen

The Easter Vigil

HYMN

The day of resurrection! Earth, tell it out abroad,
the passover of gladness, the passover of God.
From death to life eternal, from sin's dominion free,
our Christ has brought us over with hymns of victory.

Now let the heav'ns be joyful, let earth its song begin,
let all the world keep triumph and all that is therein.
Let all things, seen and unseen, their notes of gladness blend;
for Christ the Lord has risen, our joy that has no end!

Then praise we God the Father, and praise we Christ the Son,
with them the Holy Spirit, eternal Three in One;
till all the ransomed number fall down before the throne,
and honor, pow'r, and glory ascribe to God alone!
Tune: LANCASHIRE (*Lead on, O King eternal*)
or ELLACOMBE (*O day of rest and gladness*)

PSALM 42:1-2, 4; 43:3-4

As a deer longs for flowing streams,
so my soul longs for you, O God.
My soul thirsts for God,
for the living God.
When shall I come and behold the face of God?

These things I remember, as I pour out my soul:
how I went with the throng
and led them in procession to the house of God,
with glad shouts and songs of thanksgiving,
a multitude keeping festival.

O send out your light and your truth;
let them lead me;
let them bring me to your holy hill
and to your dwelling.

Then I will go to the altar of God,
to God my exceeding joy;
and I will praise you with the harp,
O God, my God.

SCRIPTURE

Gen. 1:1—2:4a	Gen. 7:1—9:17	Gen. 22:1-18
Exod. 14:10-31;15:20-21	Isa. 55:1-11	Prov. 8:1—9:6
Ezek. 36:24-28	Ezek. 37:1-14	Zeph. 3:14-20
Rom. 6:3-11	Ps. 114	Mark 16:1-8

CANTICLE

Rejoice, now,
all heavenly choirs of angels,
and celebrate the divine mysteries with exultation;
and, for the victory of so great a King,
sound the trumpet of salvation.

Exult, also, O earth,
enlightened with such radiance;
and, made brilliant by the splendor of the eternal King,
know that the ancient darkness
has been banished from all the world.

Be glad also, O mother Church,
clothed with the brightness of such a light,
and let this house resound
with the triumphant voices of the peoples.

For this indeed is the paschal feast
in which the true Lamb is slain,
by whose blood the doorposts of the faithful are made holy.

This is the night which, in ancient times,
you delivered our forebears, the children of Israel,
from the land of Egypt;
and led them, dry-shod, through the Red Sea.

This is the night in which, breaking the chains of death,
Christ arises from hell in triumph.

This is the night of which it is written:
"and the night is as clear as the day";
and, "then shall my night be turned into day."

O night truly blessed
in which heaven and earth are joined.
The Exsultet, Easter Vigil Proclamation

PRAYER

Prayers for others and ourselves
The Lord's Prayer

 O God,
who made this most holy night
to shine with the glory of the Lord's resurrection:
Stir up in your church that Spirit of adoption
which is given to us in baptism,
that we, being renewed both in body and mind,
may worship you in sincerity and truth.
Amen

O God,
you increase your church
by continuing to call all peoples to salvation.
Let the cleansing waters of baptism flow,
and by your love watch over those whom you have called;
through your Son, Jesus Christ our Lord.
Amen

BLESSING FOR MAUNDY THURSDAY

O God of love,
as your Son washed the feet of his disciples,
he revealed his undying love that would lead him to the cross.
May this simple act be a sign of our love for one another,
and our call to serve our neighbors and all those in need,
through Christ our Lord.
Amen

BLESSING FOR GOOD FRIDAY

O Christ, Lamb of God,
on this day we offer you the adoration of our hearts,
for on the cross you reveal your suffering love.
May we who celebrate the triumph of the cross,
receive the assurance of your victory over death
and the hope of resurrection,
for you live and reign for ever and ever.
Amen

BLESSING FOR EASTER EVE

God of new life,
through our baptism into Christ you have raised us with him
to the joy of the resurrection.
You have brought us through the Red Sea
and fed us with the food and drink of the promised land.
May the fire of your love renew our faith
and deepen our commitment to you,
that we might faithfully live in the covenant of our baptism,
through Christ our Lord.
Amen

Easter

*I*t is good that Easter lasts fifty days, for it will take us at least that long to explore the garden of God.

According to one of the creation stories in Genesis, the original home for human beings was a garden. But after the fall, God expelled Adam and Eve from the garden so that they could not eat the fruit of the tree of life and live forever. Throughout the history of the faithful people, there remained a longing for the garden. The prophets anticipated a time coming in the future when the desert all around them would flourish like a blossoming garden. The Song of Solomon places the lovers in a garden, and particularly Christians during the Middle Ages found this poem a metaphor of what life with God will be like. The book of Revelation, with its visions of the end time, describes a garden inside a city, as if both God's nature and human culture participate in what heaven will be.

With these biblical gardens in mind, we discover that John describes both Gethsemane, the place of Jesus' betrayal, and the location of Jesus' tomb as gardens. Of course John would do that: see the place of Jesus' death as the site of vibrant life. Thus John's Easter gospels take place in a garden, Mary of Magdala even mistaking Jesus as the gardener. It is this garden that we enjoy for the fifty days of Easter, leaving finally on Pentecost Sunday to go out preaching to all the ends of the earth.

The readings for the Fifty Days include both the stories of

Jesus' appearances to the disciples and selections from the
Gospel of John. These texts are particularly intriguing to read
during Easter, since the writer of John, although meaning
these speeches to be read by the Easter community, puts the
words in Jesus' mouth before his death. Thus we recall that
the garden we enjoy during these discourses is always also the
garden of Jesus' agony. The place of our life is the place of
Jesus' death.

While we are in the garden, we sing hymns penned
throughout the Christian centuries. With Fortunatus from
the sixth century we sing of "all the fair beauty of the earth."
With John of Damascus from the eighth century, we laud this
"queen of seasons." In an eleventh-century chant, we recall
Mary in the garden with Christ. With Martin Luther we
praise Christ as "the sun that warms and lights us." Charles
Wesley in the eighteenth century reminds us that "the sun's
eclipse is o'er." The twentieth-century "Now the green blade
rises" addresses honestly those times when "our hearts are
wintry, grieving, or in pain." These songs help us to celebrate
the springtime of the resurrection.

Easter is a fifty-day celebration; it is also the weekly celebration of meeting Christ in the breaking of the bread; it is
also the daily "dying and rising" of each baptized Christian.
The season concludes with Pentecost and the story of the
tongues of fire, Luke's way to say what John said of Easter
Sunday evening: that Christ gives to the community of
believers the Spirit of his resurrected body. Christ is now
alive in us.

While the church is enjoying the garden, so is the natural
world. During these seven weeks the Northern Hemisphere

has been adorned with forsythia, crocuses, daffodils, tulips, azaleas, dogwood, flowering fruit trees, and finally roses. The spring processes by us in one bunch of flowers after another. Days are warming, days are lengthening. People are beginning to move outside, to plan their own gardens, to tend their yards, to eat out on the patio, to pack away winter clothes. It is as if the natural and secular worlds are celebrating God's garden without realizing it.

But the fifty days of Easter do not ensure seven weeks of bliss for all the faithful. Sorrow will come, disappointment arrives. There is no security guard at the garden gates keeping death out. Herein lies yet another reason that we want Easter to last fifty days. Most folk can get all excited one or two days each year, don new clothes and enjoy the music. But we can't keep up such glee for fifty days. John's Gospel knows that, by placing both Jesus' agony and his resurrection in a garden. Many Christians will have some of these fifty days that are not at all filled with light and happiness. But the hope is that each of the fifty days will be marked by the presence of the risen Christ in each of us and within the community. In spite of every sin and sorrow, we practice the joy of the resurrection. Even in the midst of the woods, we recognize the garden, and we practice pointing out to each other the tree of life.

Praying in Easter

INVITATION

This is the feast of victory for our God.
Alleluia!

TABLE PRAYER

As you once revealed yourself
in the breaking of the bread, O risen Lord,
be with us now as we share this food and drink.
Open our eyes to recognize you in both friends and strangers,
and enlighten us with your Spirit
so that our words and actions
may be signs of hope for all people.
Amen. Alleluia.

HYMN

Alleluia! Jesus is risen!
Trumpets resounding in glorious light!
Splendor, the Lamb, heaven forever!
Oh, what a miracle God has in sight!
Refrain:
Jesus is risen and we shall arise:
Give God the glory! Alleluia!

Walking the way, Christ in the center
telling the story to open our eyes;
breaking our bread, giving us glory:
Jesus our blessing, our constant surprise. *Refrain*

Jesus the vine, we are the branches;
life in the Spirit the fruit of the tree;
heaven to earth, Christ to the people,
gift of the future now flowing to me. *Refrain*

Weeping, be gone; sorrow, be silent:
death put asunder, and Easter is bright.
Cherubim sing: "O grave, be open!"
Clothe us in wonder, adorn us in light. *Refrain*

City of God, Easter forever,
golden Jerusalem, Jesus the Lamb,
river of life, saints and archangels,
sing with creation to God the I AM! *Refrain*
Tune: EARTH AND ALL STARS

PSALM 118: 1-4, 13-18, 22-24

Give thanks, the Lord is good,
God's love is for ever!
Now let Israel say,
"God's love is for ever!"

Let the house of Aaron say,
"God's love is for ever!"
Let all who revere the Lord say,
"God's love is for ever!"

I was pushed to falling,
but the Lord gave me help.
My strength, my song is the Lord,
who has become my savior.

Glad songs of victory sound
within the tents of the just.
With right hand raised high,
the Lord strikes with force.

I shall not die but live
to tell the Lord's great deeds.
The Lord punished me severely,
but did not let me die.

The stone the builders rejected
has become the cornerstone.
This is the work of the Lord,
how wonderful in our eyes.

This is the day the Lord made,
let us rejoice and glad. [ICEL]

SCRIPTURE

See the daily readings

CANTICLE

In the morning, the Song of Zechariah (page 21)
In the evening, the Song of Mary (page 27)
At bedtime, the Song of Simeon (page 29) or

Do you not know that all of us who have been baptized
    into Christ Jesus were baptized into his death?
Therefore we have been buried with him by baptism into death,
so that, just as Christ was raised from the dead by the glory of the
    Father,
so we too might walk in newness of life.

For if we have been united with him in a death like his,
we will certainly be united with him in a resurrection like his.

We know that our old self was crucified with him
so that the body of sin might be destroyed,
and we might no longer be enslaved to sin.
For whoever has died is freed from sin.
But if we have died with Christ,
we believe that we will also live with him.

We know that Christ, being raised from the dead,
will never die again;
death no longer has dominion over him.
The death he died, he died to sin, once for all;
but the life he lives, he lives to God.

So you also must consider yourselves dead to sin
and alive to God in Christ Jesus.
       Romans 6:3-11

PRAYER

Prayers for others and ourselves
The Lord's Prayer

O God,
you gave your only Son
to suffer death on the cross for our redemption,
and by his glorious resurrection
you delivered us from the power of death.
Make us die every day to sin,
so that we may live with him forever in the joy of resurrection;
through Jesus Christ our Lord,
who lives and reigns with you and the Holy Spirit,
one God, now and forever.
Amen

THANKSGIVING FOR BAPTISM

Use this prayer throughout the Fifty Days of Easter.
Gather around a bowl of water with a burning candle set next to it.

Gracious God,
we praise you for the new life you have given us in baptism.
We thank you for the bread of life
and cup of salvation that nourish us.

Through the power of your Holy Spirit,
bless us and strengthen us in the household of faith
so that we may serve each other in peace.
Through the turning of the days
and the changing of the seasons,
hold us secure in your loving arms,
and by the light of the risen Christ
lead us at last into the presence of your unfading light.

Grant this through Jesus Christ, the resurrection and the life,
who lives and reigns with you and the Holy Spirit,
one God, now and forever.
Amen

BLESSING OF FIELDS AND GARDENS

Use this prayer when preparing the soil and planting seed or bulbs.

O God, our creator,
from the earth you bring forth fruits and vegetables,
grains and flowers, to nourish and delight us.
Grant that this land,
sustained by rain and favorable weather
and cultivated by human hands,
may bring forth an abundant harvest,
through Jesus Christ our Lord.
Amen

PRAYER TO THE HOLY SPIRIT

*Use this prayer during the last two weeks of Easter and during the week
following Pentecost Sunday.*

Come to us, Holy Spirit,
and be the source of life restored.
Send your rain upon our dusty lives.
Wash away our sin and folly.
Heal our worn and wounded spirits.
Ignite the fire of your love within our hearts.
Burn away the apathetic hold of our ancient enemy.
Loosen what is rigid within us
and guide us in safety to our final home.
Amen

BLESSING FOR MOTHERS DAY

Use this prayer on the second Sunday in May

Loving God,
as a mother gives nourishment to her children,
so you care for your faithful people.
We ask you to bless our mother
that she may be strengthened by your love.
Let the witness of her faith
be a light for all who look to her for encouragement.
May she be surrounded by our love
and honored by our reverence for her life.
Grant this through Christ our Lord.
Amen

Daily Readings and Prayers

Resurrection of the Lord

S Acts 10:34-43   Ps. 118:1-2, 14-24
      I Cor. 15:1-11   John 20:1-18
M Gen. 1:1—2:4a   **T** Ps. 33
W Mark 16:9-18   **Th** Song of Sol. 3:1-11
F I Cor. 15:35-58   **S** Ps. 118

For prayer throughout the day
    Alleluia! I have seen the Lord. *John 20:18*

A prayer for the week
    Risen Savior,
    come to us in the darkness of night
    and enlighten us with your saving light.
    Amen

Second Sunday of Easter

S Acts 4:32-35   Ps. 133
      I John 1:1—2:2   John 20:19-31
M Dan. 3:1-30   **T** Dan. 6:1-28
W Mark 12:18-27   **Th** Isa. 26:1-9
F I John 2:3-17   **S** Ps. 135

For prayer throughout the day
    My Lord and my God. *John 20:28*

A prayer for the week
    Risen Christ,
    you come to us in your word,
    the sacraments of your love,
    and the community of faith.
    Open our eyes to see your presence.
    Amen

Third Sunday of Easter

S	Acts 3:12-19		Ps. 4
	I John 3:1-7		Luke 24:36b-48
M	Exod. 24:9-18	**T**	Hosea 5:15—6:6
W	Luke 18:31-34	**Th**	Micah 4:1-5
F	I John 3:7-15	**S**	Ps. 35

For prayer throughout the day

When Christ is revealed, we shall be like him. *1 John 3:2*

A prayer for the week

Lord of peace,
you open the hearts of your disciples
to understand the scriptures.
Reveal yourself to us in your word
so that we may know your love and mercy.
Amen

Fourth Sunday of Easter

S	Acts 4:5-12		Ps. 23
	I John 3:16-24		John 10:11-18
M	Gen. 48:8-21	**T**	I Chron. 11:1-9
W	Mark 14:26-31	**Th**	Micah 7:8-20
F	I Peter 5:1-5	**S**	Ps. 23

For prayer throughout the day

O God, help us love in action and in truth. *See 1 John 3:18*

A prayer for the week

Good Shepherd,
you laid down your life
and rose again to be with your people.
Help us serve the flock you have redeemed with your blood.
Amen

Fifth Sunday of Easter

S   Acts 8:26-40   Ps. 22:25-31
         1 John 4:7-21   John 15:1-8
M   Isa. 5:1-7   **T**   Isa. 32:1-20
W   John 14:22-31   **Th**   Isa. 65:17-25
F   Gal. 5:22-26   **S**   Ps. 80

For prayer throughout the day
O God, give us the love of you that casts out fear. *See 1 John 4:18*

A prayer for the week
Compassionate God,
you call us to love others as you love us.
Through your love, may our lives bear fruit and glorify you.
Amen

Sixth Sunday of Easter

S   Acts 10:44-48   Ps. 98
         1 John 5:1-6   John 15:9-17
M   Deut. 7:1-11   **T**   Deut. 11:1-17
W   Mark 16:19-20

For prayer throughout the day
I have chosen you to bear fruit that will last. *See John 15:16*

A prayer for the week
Risen Lord,
you call us your friends.
Strengthen us in the bonds of friendship
and help us serve the stranger in need.
Amen

Ascension of the Lord

         Acts 1:1-11   Ps. 47
         Eph. 1:15-23   Luke 24:44-53
F   Rev. 1:9-18   **S**   Ps. 110

For prayer throughout the day
Spirit of God, give us wisdom. *See Ephesians 1:17*

A prayer for the week
> Lord Jesus,
> Send your Spirit upon us and your church
> so that we may continue to serve you in peace.
> Amen

Seventh Sunday of Easter

S	Acts 1:15-17, 21-26		Ps. 1
	1 John 5:9-13		John 17:6-19
M	Exod. 28:29-38	**T**	Num. 8:5-22
W	John 16:16-24	**Th**	Ezra 9:5-15
F	Acts 1:12-23	**S**	Ps. 141

For prayer throughout the day
> Come, Holy Spirit, and renew the face of the earth.

A prayer for the week
> Spirit of the living God,
> restore us, strengthen us,
> and lead us in service to all in need.
> Keep us in your truth and unite us in one hope.
> Amen

Pentecost

S	Acts 2:1-21		Ps. 104:24-34, 35b
	Rom. 8:22-27		John 15:26-27; 16:4b-15
M	Joel 2:18-29	**T**	Ezek. 37:1-14
W	John 7:37-39	**Th**	Gen. 11:1-9
F	1 Cor. 12:4-13	**S**	Ps. 104

For prayer throughout the day
> Lord, send forth your Spirit and we shall live. *See Ezekiel 37:14*

A prayer for the week
> Spirit of God,
> guide us into your truth
> so we may receive all that Jesus Christ has promised.
> Amen

Summer

*I*t is summertime and seeds are growing. Little sprouts and long vines appear, flowers are turning into fruits, and the yards and fields are alive with green. It is amazing how those seeds, which look like nothing, contain in them the mystery of the mature plant. Some seeds fail, but from dandelions to sweet corn, many seeds are flourishing, and we are glad to watch them.

The increasing warmth of the days is helping the seeds. June, July, and August go from pleasant to hot to stifling, from enlivening breezes to stultifying humidity. Whether this year brings a drought or a flood, the heat impresses itself on us until we wonder how the race survived before air conditioning. Some folk relish the heat and seek out the sunshine to soak it up. Others are enervated by it and walk on the shady side of the street. But all must somehow deal with the heat.

While seeds hurry along in their task of growth and the sun pours out its rays, most people slow down. The academic year pauses, and we discover how much of the Northern Hemisphere flows along with the school year. Millions of children, no longer in classrooms, are running around houses and through the parks. College kids are home, for better and for worse. Because it is just too hot, everyone slows down. We dress more casually. Indeed, our looser clothing marks an inner loosening, a relaxation from the rigor and tensions of the normal year's work load. The only people rushing about are those hurrying off to vacations. We hurry up to slow down, leaving our fields to cultivate other seeds.

The hope for this season of the church year is steady growth. This green season is the time that the church is to move into its Easter mission, to realize the effects of the indwelling Spirit, to be nurtured by the new life of the resurrection. The Sunday readings call us each week to deeper consideration of Jesus' ministry. Christ preaches and heals, he performs miracles and occasions misunderstandings. He does with his original followers all that he does among us today. Fitting well with the theme of growth, the readings tell of Christ as the bread of life. Like wheat growing from the sower's seeds, like grapes maturing on centuries-old vines, the word of God grows within the community. We eat, and so we live.

During this green season the church practices patience in growth. Usually the indwelling of the Spirit does not evidence itself in people by outbursts of ecstasy or by a whole city being converted in one day. No, usually the growth is small, one leaf today, one bud opening tomorrow. The tomatoes take weeks, but when they ripen and we bite into them, they are like the tomatoes that the angels serve in heaven, not like the red cardboard we buy in grocery stores in winter. But growth takes time. It is slow, so slow.

Part of awaiting growth is trust. We need to trust, not only that the seeds will actually sprout but that the seeds will grow into their intended plant. Sometimes the seeds surprise us all: the tiny seed becomes a substantial tree. We all need practice at such patience, such trust. Practicing such growth and learning such trust are easier in community than by one's self. We give one another support, assuring each other that the seed will indeed sprout, and then mature, one of these days.

In some religions, an unchanging deity sits on top of everything, untouched by anything, unmoved. But the God of the scriptures is more like a growing seed than a marble monument. The stories tell us that God has second thoughts, that God remembers mercy, that God cultivates us in new and creative ways. The Spirit of the triune God is in the community, moving and growing in ways never before imagined. The original disciples were surprised that Jesus brought life also to the outcasts and to Gentiles. Surely as the body of Christ, we must incarnate the lavish growth that God promises; summertime is a good time for growing.

Praying in Summer

INVITATION

All you green things that grow on the earth,
bless the LORD.

TABLE PRAYER

God our creator,
we give you thanks for the bounty of the earth
and your abundant love made known in Jesus Christ.
Refresh us with this food and drink
that we might care for your creation
and share its many gifts with the hungry and the needy.
Grant this through Christ our Lord.
Amen

HYMN

I sing the almighty power of God, that made the mountains rise,
that spread the flowing seas abroad and built the lofty skies.
I sing the wisdom that ordained the sun to rule the day;
the moon shines full at his command, and all the stars obey.

I sing the goodness of the Lord, that filled the earth with food;
he formed the creatures with his Word,
    and then pronounced them good.
Lord, how thy wonders are displayed, where'er I turn my eye,
if I survey the ground I tread, or gaze upon the sky!

There's not a plant or flower below, but makes thy glories known;
and clouds arise, and tempests blow, by order from thy throne;
while all that borrows life from thee is ever in thy care,
and everywhere that I could be, thou, God, art present there.
Tune: ELLACOMBE (O day of rest and gladness)

PSALM 8

Lord our God,
the whole world tells
the greatness of your name.
Your glory reaches
beyond the stars.

Even the babble of infants
declares your strength,
your power to halt
the enemy and avenger.

I see your handiwork
in the heavens:
the moon and the stars
you set in place.

What is humankind
that you remember them,
the human race
that you care for them?

You treat them like gods,
dressing them in glory and splendor.
You give them charge of the earth,
laying all at their feet:

cattle and sheep,
wild beasts,
birds of the sky,
fish of the sea,
every swimming creature.

Lord our God,
the whole world tells
the greatness of your name. [ICEL]

SCRIPTURE

See the daily readings

CANTICLE

In the morning, the Song of Zechariah (page 21)
In the evening, the Song of Mary (page 27)
At bedtime, the Song of Simeon (page 29) or

Give thanks to the Father,
who has enabled you
to share in the inheritance of the saints in the light.
He has rescued us from the power of darkness
and transferred us into the kingdom of his beloved Son,
in whom we have redemption,
the forgiveness of sins.

He is the image of the invisible God,
the firstborn of all creation;
for in him all things in heaven and on earth were created,
things visible and invisible,
whether thrones or dominions or rulers or powers—
all things have been created through him and for him.

He himself is before all things,
and in him all things hold together.

He is the head of the body, the church;
he is the beginning, the firstborn from the dead,
so that he might come to have first place in everything.

For in him
all the fullness of God was pleased to dwell,
and through him
God was pleased to reconcile to himself all things,
whether on earth or in heaven,
by making peace through the blood of his cross.
        Colossians 1:12-20

PRAYER

Prayers for others and ourselves
The Lord's Prayer

God of all life,
through the visible things of this world
you show us your power and love.
From your dwelling-place
refresh our hearts and renew the face of the earth
with the life-giving water of your Word,
until the new heaven and new earth
resound with the song of resurrection
in Jesus Christ our Lord.
Amen

PRAYER FOR TRAVELERS

Use this prayer before leaving on a journey or when moving to a new home.

When Abraham and Sarah left their home,
O God, you kept them safe until their journey's end.
You led the Hebrew people through the Red Sea
and brought them to the promised land.
With an ever-watchful eye, you cared for the Israelites
as they returned from the land of exile.
Be with us now, gracious God,
as we travel in the days ahead.
Be our companion and our strength
so that we will reach our destination in safety.
Grant this prayer through Christ our Lord.
Amen

BLESSING FOR FATHERS DAY

Use this prayer on the third Sunday in June

Gracious God,
as a father cares for his children
so you surround your faithful people with mercy.
We ask you to bless our father
that he may be strengthened by your love.
Let his faith shine forth in all his words and actions.
May he be encouraged by our affection
and always look to you, our hope for years to come.
Grant this through Christ our Lord.
Amen

THANKSGIVING FOR THE EARTH'S PRODUCE

Use this prayer whenever it is appropriate in your home

God our creator,
you feed the whole world with your goodness.
As we give you thanks for the abundance of the earth,
for seedtime and harvest,
we offer you praise for Christ, the bread of life.
Keep us faithful to his word
and lead us to share all that you give us
with the hungry, the sick, and the forgotten ones of our land.
Bless us with grateful hearts as we long for the day
when all people will be fed with the harvest of justice.
We ask this in the name of Jesus,
who is our food and drink,
now and for ever.
Amen

Daily Readings and Prayers

Trinity Sunday

S   Isa. 6:1-8   Ps. 29
      Rom. 8:12-17   John 3:1-17
M Gen. 18:1-8   **T**   Exod. 33:12-23
W Mark 4:21-25   **Th** Num. 6:22-27
F   Rev. 4:1-11   **S**   Ps. 93

For prayer throughout the day

> The earth is full of your glory, O God. *See Isaiah 6:3*

A prayer for the week

> Holy Trinity,
> we are baptized into your life.
> Open our hearts to your mysterious love
> and lead us to everlasting communion in you.
> Amen

Sunday between May 29 and June 4 (Proper 4)

S   Deut. 5:12-15   Ps. 81:1-10
      2 Cor. 4:5-12   Mark 2:23—3:6
M Exod. 20:1-11   **T**   Exod. 16:13-26
W John 5:1-18   **Th** I Sam. 21:1-6
F   Acts 17:1-9   **S**   Ps. 81

For prayer throughout the day

> I am the Lord your God.
> Open your mouth wide and I will fill it. *Psalm 81:10*

A prayer for the week

> Lord Jesus,
> help us respond to human need.
> Inspire us to imitate your love
> even when others ridicule us.
> Amen

Sunday between June 5 and 11 (Proper 5)

S Gen. 3:8-15   Ps. 130
    2 Cor. 4:13—5:1   Mark 3:20-35
M I Kings 18:17-40 **T** 2 Kings 1:1-10
W Luke 11:14-28 **Th** Isa. 26:16—27:1
F Rev. 20:1-15 **S** Ps. 74

For prayer throughout the day
Whoever does the will of God
is my brother and sister and mother. *Mark 3:35*

A prayer for the week
Lord Jesus Christ,
you have called us to be one family in your love.
Remove the divisions that separate us from each other
and unite us in common service to the world.
Amen

Sunday between June 12 and 18 (Proper 6)

S Ezek. 17:22-24   Ps. 92:1-4, 12-15
    2 Cor. 5:6-10, 14-17 Mark 4:26-34
M Ezek. 31:1-12 **T** Jer. 22:1-9
W Mark 4:1-20 **Th** Gen. 3:22-24
F Rev. 22:1-6 **S** Ps. 92

For prayer throughout the day
Make us a new creation. *See 2 Corinthians 5:17*

A prayer for the week
Saving Lord,
you died for all so that we might live for all.
Plant your kingdom's power within us
so that our lives may yield a fruitful harvest.
Amen

Sunday between June 19 and 25 (Proper 7)

S	Job 38:1-11		Ps. 107:1-3, 23-32
	2 Cor. 6:1-13		Mark 4:35-41
M	Gen. 1:1-3	**T**	Josh. 10:1-14
W	Mark 6:45-52	**Th**	2 Chron. 6:12-31
F	Acts 27:13-38	**S**	Ps. 107

For prayer throughout the day

Open our hearts wide, O Lord. *See 2 Corinthians 6:13*

A prayer for the week

Son of God,

you calmed the storm and replaced fear with wonder.

Increase our faith

so that we do not fear doing bold things in your name.

Amen

Sunday between June 26 and July 2 (Proper 8)

S	Lam. 3:23-33		Ps. 30
	2 Cor. 8:7-15		Mark 5:21-43
M	Lev. 21:1-15	**T**	Lev. 15:19-31
W	Mark 9:14-29	**Th**	2 Kings 20:1-11
F	2 Cor. 10:1-18	**S**	Ps. 6

For prayer throughout the day

Do not fear, only believe. *Mark 5:36*

A prayer for the week

God our strength,

your power went forth to heal.

Free us of our anxieties

and strengthen our trust in your love.

Amen

Sunday between July 3 and 9 (Proper 9)

S	Ezek. 2:1-5		Ps. 123
	2 Cor. 12:2-10		Mark 6:1-13
M	Jer. 16:1-13	**T**	Jer. 16:14-21
W	John 7:1-9	**Th**	Ezek. 2:6—3:11
F	2 Cor. 1:16-33	**S**	Ps. 119:73-88

For prayer throughout the day

> My grace is sufficient for you. *2 Corinthians 12:9*

A prayer for the week

> Gracious Lord,
> you heal the wounded and cast out evil.
> Strengthen us in the grace of baptism
> so that we may comfort the sick
> and struggle against all forms of evil in our world.
> Amen

Sunday between July 10 and 16 (Proper 10)

S	Amos 7:7-15		Ps. 85:8-13
	Eph. 1:3-14		Mark 6:14-29
M	Amos 2:4-16	**T**	Amos 4:6-13
W	Mark 15:33-39	**Th**	1 Kings 22:13-38
F	2 Cor. 12:11—13:4	**S**	Ps. 85

For prayer throughout the day

> Blessed be the God and Father of our Lord Jesus Christ.
> *Ephesians 1:3*

A prayer for the week

> God our Father,
> you reveal your love for us in Christ Jesus.
> Take away our apathy
> and give us grace to serve those in need.
> Amen

Sunday between July 17 and 23 (Proper 11)

S   Jer. 23:1-6   Ps. 23
       Eph. 2:11-22   Mark 6:30-34, 53-56
M   Ezek. 34:1-16   **T**   Ezek. 34:17-31
W   Luke 15:1-7   **Th** Zech. 9:14—10:2
F   Acts 20:16-38   **S**   Ps. 23

For prayer throughout the day
>   Come away and rest awhile. *Mark 6:31*

A prayer for the week
>   O God,
>   you desire to create a new humanity in Jesus Christ.
>   May we further the reconciliation that is your will
>   so that all people may find peace in the temple of the Lord's body.
>   Amen

Sunday between July 24 and 30 (Proper 12)

S   2 Kings 4:42-44   Ps. 145:10-18
       Eph. 3:14-21   John 6:1-21
M   Gen. 18:1-8   **T**   Exod. 24:1-11
W   Mark 6:35-44   **Th** Isa. 25:6-10
F   Eph. 3:1-13   **S**   Ps. 145

For prayer throughout the day
>   By your power, accomplish in us more than we imagine.
>   *See Ephesians 3:20*

A prayer for the week
>   Lord Jesus Christ,
>   you fed your people when you saw their hunger.
>   Open our eyes to the suffering of our neighbors
>   and give us strength to help those who hunger and thirst.
>   Amen

Sunday between July 31 and Aug. 6 (Proper 13)

S Exod. 16:2-4, 9-15   Ps. 78:23-29
    Eph. 4:1-16   John 6:24-35
M Num. 11:4-9   **T** Deut. 8:1-10
W Mark 8:1-10   **Th** Isa. 55:1-9
F Eph. 4:17-24   **S** Ps. 78:1-31

For prayer throughout the day
    Lord, give us the bread of life. *See John 6:34*

A prayer for the week
    Lord Jesus,
    you are the source of our skills and talents.
    Help us use them to strengthen the unity of your body, the church.
    Amen

Sunday between Aug. 7 and 13 (Proper 14)

S 1 Kings 19:4-8   Ps. 34:1-8
    Eph. 4:25—5:2   John 6:35, 41-51
M 1 Kings 17:1-16   **T** Ruth 2:1-23
W John 6:35-40   **Th** Jer. 31:1-6
F Eph. 5:3-14   **S** Ps. 78:32-72

For prayer throughout the day
    Lord, let me say only what builds up another. *See Ephesians 4:29*

A prayer for the week
    Loving Father,
    you have called us to live in the love of Christ.
    May the bread of life strengthen us
    to give our lives for the good of others.
    Amen

Sunday between Aug. 14 and 20 (Proper 15)

S	Prov. 9:1-6		Ps. 34:9-14
	Eph. 5:15-20		John 6:51-58
M	Gen. 43:1-15	**T**	Gen. 45:1-15
W	Mark 8:14-21	**Th**	Hosea 10:13—11:4
F	Acts 6:1-7	**S**	Ps. 34

For prayer throughout the day

Lord, let me make the most of my time. *See Ephesians 5:16*

A prayer for the week

Spirit of God,
you inspire us to sing with thanksgiving to God.
Give us grateful hearts to celebrate
the mystery of life at Christ's table.
Amen

Sunday between Aug. 21 and 27 (Proper 16)

S	Josh. 24:1-2a, 14-18		Ps. 34:15-22
	Eph. 6:10-20		John 6:56-69
M	Neh. 9:1-15	**T**	Neh. 9:16-31
W	John 15:16-25	**Th**	Isa. 33:13-16
F	Eph. 5:21—6:9	**S**	Ps. 80

For prayer throughout the day

Let my life proclaim the gospel of peace. *See Ephesians 6:15*

A prayer for the week

Lord Jesus,
we believe you are the holy one of God.
Stay with us and guide us in the work
you have given us to do in daily life.
Amen

Autumn

*F*or leaves, the process of getting ready to die is stunningly beautiful. North America is especially blessed with the kinds of trees that turn myriad shades of reds, purples, golds, and browns to celebrate September and October. On some trees, all the leaves turn entirely one solid color: we see the dogwood has become suddenly deep red. Others, like maples, can show the entire autumn display on a single leaf. A wooded hillside can be spectacular, a street lined with trees a golden cathedral. As they move towards death, the leaves are renewed, more alive with color than they were during spring.

For a culture like ours that dreads death, running away from it, trying to ignore it, and dressing it up so that it looks alive, the unique beauty of the dying leaves stops us up short. We thought that growing old and falling off is ugly and horrible, but here is evidence to the contrary. It is as if each single leaf writes its own colorful signature as it dies. Each leaf is renewed before it ends its days.

In September and October, the days are cooler and dusk comes earlier. Some weeks surprise us with their cold, but we know it is the cold air that makes the leaves turn color, giving brightness to the landscape.

Everyone gets a move on in the fall. There's a lot of work to be done before the year is over, and maybe we spent too much time over the summer lolling around. Schools begin again, and for the young people almost everything is new. Older people catch the spirit and buckle down to work, wearing business clothes again and putting in longer hours on the job. Perhaps we are all aware that the trees are turning, all of nature is turning, and we'd best not be left behind. There's a lot that needs renewal.

It is still the green season for the church. The life of the Spirit continues to grow. With the summer over, parish life naturally picks up. Meetings convene and classes resume. We expect to see everyone in church each Sunday. Perhaps the colder weather is animating everyone. Perhaps the colors of the trees remind us to do something beautiful before it's too late. Perhaps the readings, with their pointed stories of what life is like in the dominion of God, spur us on.

The readings tell us that Christ is renewing us from within. Our sicknesses healed, our ears opened, our blindness cured, we are inspired to holy living and to service towards others. Just as salt must stay salty to be any use, the body of Christ is to be continuously enlivened by the Spirit in order to be what it is. The opening prayer of each Sunday is a short, yet remarkably apt, petition: may we be made firm in the faith; may we order our lives by Christ's wisdom; may we have the grace to overcome our frailties and failures; may we serve God in willing obedience. Each prayer is a summary of our hope for renewal in the Spirit.

Some people find this autumn spirit of renewal quite difficult. In the light of the daily news, sadness seems the more appropriate emotion. Some people respond to autumn's lessening light with increasing depresssion. To counter this, the liturgical year works its communal strength. I need not try to get my act together all by myself. Christians are more realistic than that; we take human failure quite seriously. We need each other for renewal. Together we renew one another, and in this way each individual can find strength and refreshment. We are, after all, one body. A toe isn't likely to get renewed if it is cut off from the foot. A green maple leaf dies a boring green if it falls off the tree before September. The body together comes to its renewal, and autumn is an appropriate season to celebrate that renewal.

Praying in Autumn

INVITATION

Wisdom calls to her children: Come and eat of my food.
Give up ignorance; walk on the path of insight.
See Proverbs 9:5-6

TABLE PRAYER

We bless you, O God,
for the meal we share at this table.
Nourish our bodies with this food,
enlighten us with your holy wisdom,
and strengthen us to care for the hungry, the forgotten,
    and the lost.
We ask this in Jesus' name.
Amen

HYMN

For the fruit of all creation, thanks be to God.
For these gifts to ev'ry nation, thanks be to God.
For the plowing, sowing, reaping,
silent growth while we are sleeping,
future needs in earth's safekeeping,
thanks be to God.

In the just reward of labor, God's will is done.
In the help we give our neighbor, God's will is done.
In our worldwide task of caring
for the hungry and despairing,
in the harvests we are sharing,
God's will is done.

For the harvests of the Spirit, thanks be to God.
For the good we all inherit, thanks be to God.
For the wonders that astound us,
for the truths that still confound us,
most of all, that love has found us,
thanks be to God.
        Tune: AR HYD Y NOS (God, who made the earth and heaven)

PSALM 65:6b-14

You inspire awe, God, our savior,
hope of distant lands and waters.

Clothed in power,
you steady the mountains;
you still the roaring seas,
restless waves, raging nations.
People everywhere
stand amazed at what you do,
east and west shout for joy.

You tend and water the land.
How wonderful the harvest!
You fill your springs,
ready the seeds, prepare the grain.

You soak the furrows
and level the ridges.
With softening rain
you bless the land with growth.

You crown the year with riches.
All you touch comes alive:
untilled lands yield crops,
hills are dressed in joy,

flocks clothe the pastures,
valleys wrap themselves in grain.
They all shout for joy
and break into song. [ICEL]

SCRIPTURE

See the daily readings

CANTICLE

In the morning, the Song of Zechariah (page 21)
In the evening, the Song of Mary (page 27)
At bedtime, the Song of Simeon (page 29) or

Wisdom has built her house
and carved its seven pillars.
She has butchered the meat,
spiced the wine, and set her table.
She has dispatched her servant women.

She calls from the town heights,
"Let the simple-hearted come."
She tells the unschooled:
"Come, taste my bread,
drink my spiced wine.
Give up your ignorance and live,
walk the straight path of insight."

Wisdom begins when God is revered;
knowledge of the Holy One is insight.
Proverbs 9:1-6, 10 [ICEL]

PRAYER

Prayers for others and ourselves
The Lord's Prayer

Holy Wisdom,
you fill the earth with your love
and teach us to walk in your ways.
Inspire students and teachers as they search for you
in the wonders of creation and the works of humankind.
Help them see that all truth and insight comes from you,
the source of all things.
Welcome us all to the school of the gospel
so that we may learn to live what we confess with our lips.
Hear our prayer and come to our aid
for your will is to bless us,
both now and for ever.
Amen

O gracious God,
when you open your hand
you satisfy the desire of every living thing.
Bless the land and waters,
and the give the world a plentiful harvest.
As you show us your love and kindness
in the bounty of land and sea,
save us from the selfish use of your gifts,
so that men and women everywhere may give you thanks,
through Jesus Christ our Lord.
Amen

BLESSING FOR STUDENTS AND TEACHERS

Use this prayer at the beginning of the school year or whenever appropriate.

God our creator,
you surround us with the marvels of this world
and give us the ability to explore the mysteries of creation.
You fill the earth with the Spirit of wisdom
and inspire us to search for the truth.
You have sent us prophets and teachers
as witnesses to your love for us.
You have come among us in Jesus Christ
to teach us your saving truth by word and example.

Help us to enjoy our learning together
and enable us to take delight in exploration.
Give us patience in our studies
and strength to meet new challenges.
We make this prayer in the name of Jesus,
who is the way, the truth, and the life,
now and for ever.
Amen

BLESSING FOR PETS AND ANIMALS

Use this prayer on St. Francis Day, October 4, or whenever it is appropriate.

Gracious God,
in your love you created us in your image
and made us stewards of the animals
that live in the skies, the earth, and the sea.
Bless us in our care for our pet/s (animal/s).
Help us recognize your power and wisdom
in the variety of creatures that live in our world,
and hear our prayer for all that suffer
overwork, hunger, and ill-treatment.
Protect your creatures
and guard them from all evil,
now and for ever.
Amen

Daily Readings and Prayers

Sunday between Aug. 28 and Sept. 3 (Proper 17)

S	Deut. 4:1-2, 6-9		Ps. 15
	James 1:17-27		Mark 7:1-8, 14-15, 21-23
M	Exod. 32:1-14	**T**	Exod. 32:15-35
W	Mark 7:9-23	**Th**	Deut. 4:21-40
F	James 1:1-16	**S**	Ps. 38

For prayer throughout the day
> Let me be a doer of the word and not only a hearer. *See James 1:22*

A prayer for the week
> Living God,
> you call us to live our faith in word and deed.
> Deliver us from religious hypocrisy
> and bless our service for those less fortunate than ourselves.
> Amen

Sunday between Sept. 4 and 10 (Proper 18)

S	Isa. 35:4-7a		Ps. 146
	James 2:1-10, 14-17		Mark 7:24-37
M	Isa. 38:1-8	**T**	Isa. 38:9-22
W	Mark 11:12-14, 20-25	**Th**	Josh. 6:1-21
F	Heb. 11:29—12:2	**S**	Ps. 145

For prayer throughout the day
> Be strong, do not fear! Here is your God. *Isaiah 35:4*

A prayer for the week
> Your power heals those who trust in you, O God.
> Draw near and heal those who cry to you.
> Amen

Sunday between Sept. 11 and 17 (Proper 19)

S   Isa. 50:4-9a   Ps. 116:1-9
      James 3:1-12   Mark 8:27-38
M Isa. 42:1-4   **T**   Isa. 49:1-6
W John 7:25-39   **Th** Isa. 52:13—53:12
F   James 2:17-26   **S**   Ps. 116

For prayer throughout the day
>You are the Christ. *Mark 8:29*

A prayer for the week
>Lord Jesus Christ,
>open our ears
>so that we might hear you speak to us.
>Amen

Sunday between Sept. 18 and 24 (Proper 20)

S   Jer. 11:18-20   Ps. 54
      James 3:13—4:3, 7-8a Mark 9:30-37
M 1 Sam. 3:2-18   **T**   2 Kings 5:1-14
W John 8:21-38   **Th** Jer. 1:4-10
F   James 4:8—5:6   **S**   Ps. 139

For prayer throughout the day
>Wisdom is full of mercy. *James 3:17*

A prayer for the week
>Lord Jesus,
>give us the wisdom to recognize your presence,
>in the stranger, the friend, the outcast.
>Amen

Sunday between Sept. 25 and Oct. 1 (Proper 21)

S	Num. 11:4-6, 10-16, 24-29		Ps. 19:7-14
	James 5:13-20		Mark 9:38-50
M	Exod. 18:13-27	**T**	Deut. 1:1-18
W	Matt. 5:1-16	**Th**	Zech. 10:1-12
F	James 5:10-12	**S**	Ps. 19

For prayer throughout the day

Lord, let us be at peace with one another. *See Mark 9:50*

A prayer for the week

Jesus, teacher of your people,

may we never be an obstacle to the faith of others.

Amen

Sunday between Oct. 2 and 8 (Proper 22)

S	Gen. 2:18-24		Ps. 8
	Heb. 1:1-4; 2:5-12		Mark 10:2-16
M	Deut. 22:13-30	**T**	Deut. 24:1-15
W	Matt. 5:17-32	**Th**	Jer. 3:6-14
F	Heb. 3:7—4:7	**S**	Ps. 45

For prayer throughout the day

God speaks to us through the Son. *See Hebrews 1:2*

A prayer for the week

Lord our God,

help us to receive your kingdom as little children,

trusting in your mercy and grace.

Amen

Sunday between Oct. 9 and 15 (Proper 23)

S   Amos 5:6-7, 10-15   Ps. 90:12-17
     Heb. 4:12-16   Mark 10:17-31
M Deut. 5:1-20   **T** Deut. 5:21-33
W Mark 12:13-17   **Th** Micah 7:1-7
F Heb. 5:11-12   **S** Ps. 90

For prayer throughout the day
> Lord Jesus, give us mercy in time of need. *See Hebrews 4:16*

A prayer for the week
> Jesus,
> your grace is sufficent for each day.
> Strengthen us to live your gospel in daily life.
> Amen

Sunday between Oct. 16 and 22 (Proper 24)

S   Isa. 53:4-12   Ps. 91:9-16
     Heb. 5:1-10   Mark 10:35-45
M I Sam. 8:1-18   **T** I Sam. 10:17-25
W Matt. 22:23-33   **Th** Prov. 10:28—11:2
F Heb. 6:1-20   **S** Ps. 81

For prayer throughout the day
> Jesus, help us to deal gently with others. *See Hebrews 5:2*

A prayer for the week
> Christ our high priest,
> you offered up cries and tears
> to the one who could save you from death.
> Give us strength to drink your cup
> in service to the needy and the lost.
> Amen

Sunday between Oct. 23 and 29 (Proper 25)

S Jer. 31:7-9   Ps. 126
       Heb. 7:23-28   Mark 10:46-52
M Lam. 1:11-18   **T** Lam. 3:40-60
W Mark 8:22-26   **Th** Jer. 33:1-11
F Heb. 7:1-25   **S** Ps. 142

For prayer throughout the day

Jesus, Son of David, have mercy on me. *Mark 10:47*

A prayer for the week

Jesus,

you gave the blind man his sight.

Give us the light to see you clearly

and to follow you with sincerity of heart.

Amen

November

*T*hank God for evergreen trees. Can you imagine how bleak November would look without those trees and bushes that retain their lively green all winter long?

In the Northern Hemisphere, November marks the dying of the landscape and the cooling of the temperature. All the autumn colors have sunk down to a dull brown. Night comes earlier and earlier, and the wind can be downright nasty. But as the earth looks more and more dead, the evergreens show off their greens, greys, yellows, tans, and blues: we had not realized how many shades of green there are. Although many stores are already decorated for Christmas, the mood of November is not expansive, but constrained. Things are preparing for the winter. November reminds us that like the leaves, we cannot escape death. It is all around us, and it is in us.

During November the liturgical year faces death honestly. The month begins with All Saints Day, the remembrance of all those dead Christians not famous enough to have their individual festal day, but as baptized members of our own body, far too important to be forgotten. Like the evergreen trees in November, the lively hymns we sing hope for life in heaven. The promise is both for now and for the future: as did Christ, so will we all conquer the grave and live with God.

The Sunday Gospel readings move on to proclaim the end time. Thus the readings are particularly contemporary. Anyone who stays abreast of the news knows that apocalyptic cults are rampant these days. Apparently, as happened in the

Western world in the decade before the year 1000, these years at the turn of the millenium excite people's imagination to predict, or at least to anticipate, the end of the world. Whether by human horror or natural cataclysm or act of God, the end is coming, say Christian and non-Christian groups alike. Usually, just like in the apocalyptic readings of the Gospels and the book of Revelation, the end is described in catastrophic terms, with the frightened inner circle being the only people who will survive its ravages. Some disturbed persons believe it is their task to bring on the end; others live in dread of its inevitability.

Christians can offer a unique slant to apocalyptic fear in the bold declaration of God's steadfast mercy. The risen Christ stands with us as we, his body, call the entire world into that life of God. In the Gospel reading we hear the evangelists' prophecies of coming wars and earthquakes and famines. But then in the sharing of the Peace we greet one another with the Easter greeting—"peace be with you"—and in the eucharist we share the meal that we believe is only the first course of the feast of heaven. Our communal rituals of shared prayer and shared food are like an evergreen tree standing confidently in a barren field. We hear and taste and trust in God's mercy in the face of death.

The year concludes with Christ the King, with its message that God's life survives death, that Christ's reign from the cross is the only true power or might in this world. Christ who has died now reigns from the throne of God. In the place of the cross is an evergreen.

Despite the popularity of movies about horror and destruction, despite the morbid cast that characterizes the daily news, much in our culture avoids death, pretending it won't come our way. More and more of our relatives die in the hospital, and the dead body is removed by professionals who dress it up to look just fine. Usually the mourners are already in their cars leaving the cemetery before the body is actually buried, lowered into the ground and covered over with dirt, so much do we avoid looking death and the grave in the face.

November gives the Christian community a time to practice getting ready to die. This is particularly painful to do alone, and so together we recall the lives of the baptized saints of God. Together we think about the death of everyone, perhaps even someday the death of the world itself. Yet Christians see in the death of Christ the beginning of life.

It is not that the church should become a cult of the dead—far from it. But because of the cross, we need not fear death, avoiding it or disguising it. We need not use euphemisms—"passed away"—to circumvent the truth. We can face death straight on and walk through it into the mystery of God. We can help shovel the dirt into the grave because we know that like the evergreen we will live. For Christ who calls us together during November has already died. "Christ has died, Christ is risen, Christ will come again" we proclaim every Sunday at the table. And so we eat, that we may live now, and after death as well.

Praying in November

INVITATION

The Lamb will be our shepherd
and guide us to the waters of life. *See Revelation 22:1-2*

TABLE PRAYER

God of the harvest,
we give you thanks for the blessings of this table.
May this meal be a foretaste of heaven's feast,
where all the hungry shall be fed
and we will join our beloved dead
in praise of your eternal mercy.
We ask this in the name of our Lord Jesus Christ,
whose coming is certain and whose day draws near.
Amen

HYMN

Sing with all the saints in glory,
sing the resurrection song!
Death and sorrow, earth's dark story,
to the former days belong.
All around the clouds are breaking,
soon the storms of time shall cease;
in God's likeness we awaken,
knowing everlasting peace.

Oh, what glory, far exceeding
all that eye has yet perceived!
Holiest hearts for ages pleading
never that full joy conceived.
God has promised, Christ prepares it,
there on high our welcome waits.
Ev'ry humble spirit shares it,
Christ has passed the eternal gates.

Life eternal! Heav'n rejoices:
Jesus lives who once was dead.
Shout with joy, O deathless voices!
Child of God, lift up your head!
Life eternal! Oh, what wonders
crowd on faith; what joy unknown,
when, amid earth's closing thunders,
saints shall stand before the throne!

Tune: HYMN TO JOY *(Joyful, joyful we adore thee)*

PSALM 116: 5-16

Kind and faithful is the Lord,
gentle is our God.
The Lord shelters the poor,
raises me from the dust.
Rest once more, my heart,
for you know the Lord's love.

God rescues me from death,
wiping my tears,
steadying my feet.
I walk with the Lord
in this land of the living.

I believe, even as I say,
"I am afflicted."
I believe, even though I scream,
"Everyone lies!"

What gift can ever repay
God's gift to me?
I raise the cup of freedom
as I call on God's name!
I fulfill my vows to you, Lord,
standing before your assembly.

Lord, you hate to see
your faithful ones die.
I beg you, Lord, hear me:
it is I, the servant you love,
I, the child of your servant.
You freed me from death's grip. [ICEL]

SCRIPTURE

See the daily readings

CANTICLE

In the morning, the Song of Zechariah (page 21)
In the evening, the Song of Mary (page 27)
At bedtime, the Song of Simeon (page 29) or

We thank you, Lord,
God and ruler of all,
who is and who was.
You have claimed your power
and begun to reign.

When the nations raged
your anger stirred.
Then was the moment
to judge the dead,
to reward your servants, the prophets,
to honor your holy ones
who honored your name,
small and great alike.

Now is salvation,
the power and reign of God;
the Christ holds command.
For the one who accused the saints
day and night before God
has now been driven out.

They won the battle
by the blood of the Lamb
and by the power of their witness
despite the threat of death.

Citizens of heaven, rejoice.
                Revelation 11:17-18; 12:10b-12a [ICEL]

PRAYER

Prayers for others and ourselves
The Lord's Prayer

O God,
our help in ages past and our hope for years to come:
we give you thanks for all your faithful people
who have followed the light of your word
throughout the centuries into our time and place . . .
[individual names may be spoken].
As we remember these people,
strengthen us to follow Christ through this world
until we are carried into the harvest of eternal life
where suffering and death shall be no more.
Hear our prayer in the name of the Lord Jesus,
our good and gracious shepherd,
who lives and reigns with you and the Holy Spirit,
one God, now and for ever.
Amen

Almighty God,
your generous goodness comes to us new every day.
By the work of your Spirit
lead us to acknowledge your goodness,
give thanks for your benefits,
and serve you in willing obedience,
through your Son, Jesus Christ our Lord.
Amen

Jesus,
remember me
when you come into your kingdom.
      Luke 23:42

PRAYER FOR PEACE AT THE LAST

O Lord,
support us all the day long of this troubled life,
until the shadows lengthen and the evening comes
and the busy world is hushed,
the fever of life is over, and our work is done.
Then, Lord, in your mercy,
grant us a safe lodging, and a holy rest,
and peace at the last;
through Jesus Christ our Lord.
Amen

PRAYER FOR THOSE NEAR DEATH

Use this prayer when someone is near death. Speak the name of the person and then say,

We entrust you to God who created you.
May you return to the one who formed us out of the dust of the
  earth.
Surrounded by the angels and triumphant saints,
may Christ come to meet you
as you go forth from this life.

Christ, the Lord of glory, who was crucified for you,
bring you freedom and peace.

Christ, the High Priest, who has forgiven all your sins,
keep you among his people.

Christ, the Son of God, who died for you,
show you the glories of his eternal kingdom.

Christ, the Good Shepherd,
enfold you with his tender care.

May you see your redeemer face to face
and enjoy the sight of God forever.

Amen

THANKSGIVING FOR THE FAITHFUL DEPARTED

Use this prayer when visiting the grave of a loved one.

O God,
we remember with thanksgiving
those who have loved and served you on earth,
who now rest from their labors
[especially . . .].
Keep us in union with all your saints
and bring us with them to the joyous feast of heaven,
through Jesus Christ our Lord.
Amen

Rest eternal grant *him/her*, O Lord;
and let light perpetual shine upon *him/her*.

Daily Readings and Prayers

Sunday between Oct. 30 and Nov. 5 (Proper 26)

S Deut. 6:1-9   Ps. 119:1-8
     Heb. 9:11-14   Mark 12:28-34
M Deut. 6:10-25   **T** Micah 6:1-8
W Mark 12:35-37 **Th** Isa. 58:1-9
F Heb. 8:1-13   **S** Ps. 51

For prayer throughout the day
> Lord, help me love you with my whole heart. *See Mark 12:30*

A prayer for the week
> Lord Jesus,
> help us to love you
> through service to our neighbors in need.
> Amen

Sunday between Nov. 6 and 12 (Proper 27)

S 1 Kings 17:8-16   Ps. 146
     Heb. 9:24-28   Mark 12:38-44
M Ruth 1:1-22   **T** Ruth 4:7-22
W Matt. 23:1-28 **Th** Deut. 24:17-22
F Heb. 9:15-24   **S** Ps. 94

For prayer throughout the day
> I will praise the LORD as long as I live. *Psalm 146:2*

A prayer for the week
> Lord Jesus,
> you warn us not to practice goodness
> for the reward others give us.
> Teach us true poverty of spirit
> and generosity of heart.
> Amen

Sunday between Nov. 13 and 19 (Proper 28)

S	Dan. 12:1-3		Ps. 16
	Heb. 10:11-14, 19-25		Mark 13:1-8
M	Dan. 4:1-18	**T**	Dan. 4:19-37
W	Mark 13:9-23	**Th**	Zech. 12:1—13:1
F	Heb. 10:1-10	**S**	Ps. 83

For prayer throughout the day
> Lord, help my unbelief. *See Hebrews 10:23*

A prayer for the week
> Lord Jesus,
> you call us to prepare for the last day.
> Give us strong faith,
> firm hope,
> and loving hearts.
> Amen

Christ the King/Reign of Christ (Proper 29)

S	Dan. 7:9-10, 13-14		Ps. 93
	Rev. 1:4b-8		John 18:33-37
M	Dan. 7:1-14	**T**	Dan. 7:15-28
W	John 16:25-33	**Th**	Ezek. 28:20-26
F	Rev. 11:15-19	**S**	Ps. 102

For prayer throughout the day
> Jesus, help us recognize your reign in human life.

A prayer for the week
> Lord Jesus,
> we praise you as our king
> who reigns from the throne of the cross.
> Look upon all the suffering people of the world
> and come to them with your mercy.
> Amen

Church year calendar for Year of Mark (Cycle B)

Day	1996–1997	1999–2000	2002–2003	2005–2006	2008–2009
First Sunday in Advent	Dec. 1, 1996	Nov. 28, 1999	Dec. 1, 2002	Nov. 27, 2005	Nov. 30, 2008
Baptism of the Lord	Jan. 12, 1997	Jan. 9, 2000	Jan. 12, 2003	Jan. 8, 2006	Jan. 11, 2009
		First Sunday after the Epiphany			
Transfiguration of the Lord	Feb. 9	Mar. 5	Mar. 2	Feb. 26	Feb. 22
		Last Sunday after the Epiphany			
Ash Wednesday	Feb. 12	Mar. 8	Mar. 5	Mar. 1	Feb. 25
First Sunday in Lent	Feb. 16	Mar. 12	Mar. 9	Mar. 5	Mar. 1
Passion Sunday	Mar. 23	Apr. 16	Apr. 13	Apr. 9	Apr. 5
Maundy Thursday	Mar. 27	Apr. 20	Apr. 17	Apr. 13	Apr. 9
Good Friday	Mar. 28	Apr. 21	Apr. 18	Apr. 14	Apr. 10
Easter Vigil	Mar. 29	Apr. 22	Apr. 19	Apr. 15	Apr. 11
Resurrection of the Lord	Mar. 30	Apr. 23	Apr. 20	Apr. 16	Apr. 12
	Easter Day				
Ascension of the Lord	May 8	June 1	May 29	May 25	May 21
Day of Pentecost	May 18	June 11	June 8	June 4	May 31
Trinity Sunday	May 25	June 18	June 15	June 11	June 7
	First Sunday after Pentecost				
S. btwn. May 29 and 4 (Pr. 4)	June 1				
S. btwn. June 5 and 11 (Pr. 5)	June 8				
S. btwn. June 12 and 18 (Pr. 6)	June 15			June 18	June 14
S. btwn. June 19 and 25 (Pr. 7)	June 22	June 25	June 22	June 25	June 21
S. btwn. June 26 and July 2 (Pr. 8)	June 29	July 2	June 29	July 2	June 28

Day	1996–1997	1999–2000	2002–2003	2005–2006	2008–2009
S. btwn. July 3 and 9 (Pr. 9)	July 6	July 9	July 6	July 9	July 5
S. btwn. July 10 and 16 (Pr. 10)	July 13	July 16	July 13	July 16	July 12
S. btwn. July 17 and 23 (Pr. 11)	July 20	July 23	July 20	July 23	July 19
S. btwn. July 24 and 30 (Pr. 12)	July 27	July 30	July 27	July 30	July 26
S. btwn. July 31 and Aug. 6 (Pr. 13)	Aug. 3	Aug. 6	Aug. 3	Aug. 6	Aug. 2
S. btwn. Aug. 7 and 13 (Pr. 14)	Aug. 10	Aug. 13	Aug. 10	Aug. 13	Aug. 9
S. btwn. Aug. 14 and 20 (Pr. 15)	Aug. 17	Aug. 20	Aug. 17	Aug. 20	Aug. 16
S. btwn. Aug. 21 and 27 (Pr. 16)	Aug. 24	Aug. 27	Aug. 24	Aug. 27	Aug. 23
S. btwn. Aug. 28 and Sept. 3 (Pr. 17)	Aug. 31	Sept. 3	Aug. 31	Sept. 3	Aug. 30
S. btwn. Sept. 4 and 10 (Pr. 18)	Sept. 7	Sept. 10	Sept. 7	Sept. 10	Sept. 6
S. btwn. Sept. 11 and 17 (Pr. 19)	Sept. 14	Sept. 17	Sept. 14	Sept. 17	Sept. 13
S. btwn. Sept. 18 and 24 (Pr. 20)	Sept. 21	Sept. 24	Sept. 21	Sept. 24	Sept. 20
S. btwn. Sept. 25 and Oct. 1 (Pr. 21)	Sept. 28	Oct. 1	Sept. 28	Oct. 1	Sept. 27
S. btwn. Oct. 2 and 8 (Pr. 22)	Oct. 5	Oct. 8	Oct. 5	Oct. 8	Oct. 4
S. btwn. Oct. 9 and 15 (Pr. 23)	Oct. 12	Oct. 15	Oct. 12	Oct. 15	Oct. 11
S. btwn. Oct. 16 and 22 (Pr. 24)	Oct. 19	Oct. 22	Oct. 19	Oct. 22	Oct. 18
S. btwn. Oct. 23 and 29 (Pr. 25)	Oct. 26	Oct. 29	Oct. 26	Oct. 29	Oct. 25
S. btwn. Oct. 30 and Nov. 5 (Pr. 26)	Nov. 2	Nov. 5	Nov. 2	Nov. 5	Nov. 1
S. btwn. Nov. 6 and 12 (Pr. 27)	Nov. 9	Nov. 12	Nov. 9	Nov. 12	Nov. 8
S. btwn. Nov. 13 and 19 (Pr. 28)	Nov. 16	Nov. 19	Nov. 16	Nov. 19	Nov. 15
Christ the King	Nov. 23	Nov. 26	Nov. 23	Nov. 26	Nov. 22
	Last Sunday after Pentecost				
Day of Thanksgiving—Canada	Oct. 13	Oct. 9	Oct. 13	Oct. 9	Oct. 12
Day of Thanksgiving—U.S.A.	Nov. 27	Nov. 23	Nov. 27	Nov. 23	Nov. 26

Acknowledgments

Unless otherwise noted, songs, prayers, and blessings that are published in this collection are copyrighted by Augsburg Fortress.

Scripture quotations, except for those psalms noted as ICEL, are from the New Revised Standard Version Bible, copyright © 1989 Division of Christian Education of the National Council of the Churches of Christ in the United States of America. Used by permission.

Psalm quotations and canticles noted as ICEL are from the English translation of the psalms from the *Liturgical Psalter*, copyright © 1994, 1995, International Committee on English in the Liturgy, Inc. All rights reserved. Used by permission.

Prayers acknowledged as *LBW* are copyright © 1978 *Lutheran Book of Worship*.

Upon Waking

I give thanks to you, my heavenly Father: *A Contemporary Translation of Luther's Small Catechism*, tr. Timothy J. Wengert, copyright © 1994 Augsburg Fortress.

This is the feast of victory for our God: para. John Arthur, *LBW.*

Holy God, mighty Lord, gracious Father: *LBW*

Prayer in the Morning

Awake, O sleeper: Text by F. Bland Tucker, copyright © 1980 Augsburg Publishing House.

Blessed are you, Lord, the God of Israel (Song of Zechariah): The English translation of the Benedictus prepared by the English Language Liturgical Consultation (ELLC), 1988.

O Lord, almighty and everlasting God: *LBW*

At Midday

Blessed Savior, at this hour you hung upon the cross: Collect from Noonday Prayer, The Book of Common Prayer (1979 edition).

Prayer in the Evening

Light of undying glory, shine: Text copyright © James Quinn, SJ. Used by permission of Selah Publishing Co., Inc.

My soul proclaims the greatness of the Lord (Song of Mary): The English translation of the Magnificat prepared by the English Language Liturgical Consultation (ELLC), 1988.

At Bedtime

Into your hands, O Lord: *LBW*

Now, Lord, you let your servant go in peace (Song of Simeon): The English translation of the Nunc Dimittis prepared by the English Language Liturgical Consultation (ELLC), 1988.

Visit this house: Collect from Compline, The Book of Common Prayer (1979 edition), alt.

I give thanks to you, my heavenly Father: *A Contemporary Translation of Luther's Small Catechism,* tr. Timothy J. Wengert, copyright © 1994 Augsburg Fortress.

Bedtime Prayer with Children

Go, my children, with my blessing: Text copyright © 1983 Jaroslav J. Vajda. Used by permission.

Children of the heavenly Father: Text copyright © 1978 *Lutheran Book of Worship.*

All night, all day: Text, African American spiritual; public domain.

Sun of my soul: Text by John Keble, 1820, *Christian Year,* 1827; public domain.

Thy holy wings: Text by Gracia Grindal, copyright © 1994 Selah Publishing Co., Inc. All rights reserved. Used by permission.

The King of love my shepherd is: Text by Henry W. Baker; public domain.

Sunday Morning

On this day, the first of days: Text, *Die parente temporum; Carcassone Breviary,* 1745; tr. by Henry William Baker, *Hymns Ancient and Modern,* alt.; public domain.

We praise you, O God (Te Deum): The English translation of the Te Deum Laudamus prepared by the English Language Liturgical Consultation (ELLC), 1988.

Holy God, mighty Lord, we give you thanks: *LBW,* alt.

Sunday Evening

We bless you, O Lord our God: *LBW,* alt.

Abide with me: Text by Henry F. Lyte; public domain.

The Prayers of Christians

Gloria Patri: The English translation of the Gloria Patri prepared by the English Language Liturgical Consultation (ELLC), 1988.

The Apostles' Creed: The English translation of the Apostles' Creed prepared by the English Language Liturgical Consultation (ELLC), 1988.

Sanctus: The English translation of the Sanctus prepared by the English Language Liturgical Consultation (ELLC), 1988.

The Lord's Prayer: The English translation of the Lord's Prayer prepared by the English Language Liturgical Consultation (ELLC), 1988.

Lamb of God: The English translation of the Agnus Dei prepared by the English Language Liturgical Consultation (ELLC), 1988.

Advent

The King shall come: John Brownlie

O Lord, how shall I meet you: Text by Paul Gerhardt; tr. Catherine Winkworth, alt.; public domain.

O come, O come, Emmanuel (The O-Antiphons): *Keeping Advent and Christmastime*, Liturgy Training Publications. Used by permission.

Christmas

Oh, come, all ye faithful: Text attr. John F. Wade, tr. composite; public domain.

Glory to God in the highest: The English translation of the Gloria in Excelsis prepared by the English Language Liturgical Consultation (ELLC), 1988.

Almighty God, you have filled us with the new light: *LBW*

Epiphany

Songs of thankfulness and praise: Text by Christopher Wordsworth; public domain.

Lord God, on this day you revealed your Son: *LBW*

Gracious Father, we pray for your holy catholic Church: William Laud; public domain.

Lent

Restore in us, O God: Text by Carl P. Daw, Jr., copyright © 1989 Hope Publishing Co., Carol Stream, IL 60188. All rights reserved. Used by permission.

The Three Days

O Jesus, joy of loving hearts: Text attr. Bernard of Clairvaux; tr. Ray Palmer, alt.; public domain.

Lord God, in a wonderful sacrament: *LBW*

The royal banners forward go: Venantius Honorius Fortunatus, st. 1–3; source unknown, st. 4; tr. John M. Neale; public domain.

Rejoice, O life-bearing Cross: Exaltation of the cross from the Orthodox liturgy; public domain.

The day of resurrection: Text by John of Damascus; tr. John M. Neale, alt.; public domain.

Rejoice, now, all heavenly choirs of angels: *LBW*

O God, who made this most holy night to shine: The Book of Common Prayer

O God, you increase your church: *LBW*

Easter

Alleluia! Jesus is risen: Text by Herbert F. Brokering, copyright © 1995 Augsburg Fortress.

O God, you gave your only Son: *LBW*

Summer

I sing the almighty power of God: Text by Isaac Watts; public domain.

Autumn

For the fruit of all creation: Text by Fred Pratt Green, copyright © 1970 Hope Publishing Co., Carol Stream, IL 60188. All rights reserved. Used by permission.

November

Sing with all the saints in glory: Text by William J. Irons, alt.; public domain.

Almighty God, your generous goodness: *LBW*

O Lord, support us all the day long: From a sermon by John Cardinal Newman; public domain.

We entrust you to God: *Occasional Services,* copyright © 1982 by Association of Evangelical Lutheran Churches, Lutheran Church in America, The American Lutheran Church, The Evangelical Lutheran Church of Canada

O God, we remember with thanksgiving: *LBW*